To the *soror mystica* in every woman — the fire that cannot be contained or extinguished, only channeled through the vessel of her being. To the women who don't know where to begin, or may have lost their way: may the light of our hearts lead you home to your soul. I see you, I believe in you, and there is a way waiting for you; listen to the call of the wild, and it will help you find your way back to enchantment.

CONTENTS

INTRODUCTION
Melissa Kim Corter ix

L.E.A.P. INTO THE LIFE OF YOUR DREAMS
Stephanie Angle 1

TRAVELING THE ROADS OF PROSPERITY
Indhu Athreya 9

THE MYSTERY OF MONEY
Erin Christine 15

TENDING TO A PROSPEROUS SOUL
Melissa Kim Corter 21

WHEN PROSPERITY CALLS, HOW WILL YOU ANSWER?
Vicki L. Dobbs 29

PROSPERITY IS IN THE LIGHT OF A WILD WOMAN
Lisa Eleni 37

MY DANCE WITH PROSPERITY
Rachel Elizabeth 43

QUICKSAND
Sandy Hanshaw 49

SPIRITUAL SALT AND PEPPER PROSPERITY
Maribel "Belle" Hernandez 55

SOULFULLY ABUNDANT
    Patricia Horton 63

LIVE YOUR PROSPEROUS LIFE
    Melissa Jones 69

THE GIFT OF MY BEAUTIFUL WHISPERS
    Amy Kokoles 77

LET GO AND PROSPER
    Ghene't Lee-Yong 83

THE AUDACITY TO BELIEVE
    Amber Marie 91

FINDING THE GIFTS IN GRIEF & LOSS
    Paula Meyer 97

SOUL FREEDOM
    Sherri "Shaw" Morgan 103

PATHWAY TO ABUNDANCE
    Pat Mork 109

THE COSMIC FLOW OF PROSPERITY
    Janice B. Noehulani 115

THE FREEDOM OF FEELING IT ALL
    Jessica Ott 125

PROSPERITY OF EXPERIENTIAL CONNECTION:
LIVING LIFE IN PURPOSEFUL FLOW
    Lizbeth Rizzo 131

WHEEL OF PROSPERITY
  Heidi Royter 139

LIVING A FULFILLED LIFE
  GG Rush 147

SURRENDER AND ALLOW AND THE UNIVERSE WILL RESPOND
  Betty Skinner 153

ALTAR & SEX MAGICK
  Rachel Srinivasan 159

OPENING DOORS TO ABUNDANCE
  Cynthia Stoneman 165

ALL ABOARD! DESTINATION: NEW EARTH
  Brandi Strieter 171

PROSPERITY AS A WAY OF LIFE
  Shanda Trofe 179

THE MAGIC OF AWARENESS
  Julie Tufte 185

POWER OF THE MIND
  Amie Wade 191

LOVE CREATES PROSPERITY
  Jennifer Wheeler 199

A BARN, A TREE, AND ME
  Bobbi Williams 205

INNER PEACE IS CURRENCY
　　Alesha Anne Wilson... 213

PRACTICAL PROSPERITY
　　Becky Woods... 221

INTRODUCTION
Melissa Kim Corter

For many years I hid my magic and downplayed success, spiritual gifts, celebrations, and joyful experiences. I was cut down and bullied; the women around me were jealous and hateful and, worst of all, some of them were family. As a young, intuitive, and deeply sensitive child, I unknowingly took on the emotions of others. Unconsciously I decided there must be something wrong with me, so I stopped sharing. I also stopped wondering, playing, celebrating, believing, and dreaming. My enchanted world crumbled and I drifted from the "knowing" and magic of my soul.

When amazing and unexpected windfalls came my way, there was an instinctual desire to suppress the joy and reflected guilt instead. Money seemed to arrive when tragedy struck; the influx of opportunities, resources, connections, and even praise all felt tethered to loss on some level; receiving had become unsafe.

It was as if the good should feel shameful, so patterns of unworthiness took root and the magic turned to fear and despair. Everything was hard and took an enormous amount of effort, and even then achievements were short-lived in silence, as I feared the backlash of judgement I would receive if they knew.

Those days are thankfully long gone and have become the backbone of my mission, the reason why prosperity and celebration are anchored into my teachings and mentoring of other women.

This book is filled with amazing wise, wild, women who share my desire to live an enchanted life and connect you to the prosperity soaked in every ounce of this world and Universe.

May their stories, tips, formulas, and wisdom awaken and connect you to the energy of prosperity. We're here holding the spaces of these pages, inviting you to join us in sharing the most potent medicine of all: the reclamation of enchantment and *being enough*.

L.E.A.P. INTO THE LIFE OF YOUR DREAMS

Stephanie Angle

Have you ever found yourself sitting in your car screaming, "Enough is enough!!!!" Do you find yourself standing in the shower, letting the flowing water conceal your tears as you sob yourself into another day at work? Do you know deep down in your heart and soul that you were meant to be so much more in this world?

I have experienced this rollercoaster of emotions. I have dwelt in the darkness of physical and mental destruction, all the while knowing that I was meant for something larger than the life I was currently leading. There have been days when I sobbed in the shower, lost control of my emotions during lunch, and bawled my eyes out in bed just thinking about everything the next day would hold.

I dreaded each day that I was going to have to go to my job because I knew that I was supposed to be somewhere else, doing something else. Each day it was harder and harder to motivate myself. I was sick and tired of being sick and tired of my situation.

Time ticked away as I continued to follow the advice of well-meaning family members, colleagues, and friends. I rationalized staying in my position because of the medical benefits, stability of a salary and, eventually, the retirement benefits. Hour by hour, day by day, month by month, and year by year, I brushed aside the internal conflict between doing what was expected by friends, family, and colleagues, and what my instincts and intuition were pulling me toward. I listened to all the "What ifs," "Whys," and "You shoulds" while watching others taking leaps toward their dreams. My mind and body were in constant conflict, causing me to spiral deeper into the darkness and despair.

It has taken me a while to realize that my time on this earth was given to me to make an impact in the lives of others and lead them out of their darkness into the lives of their dreams. My legacy is leading the way for others to begin their journey. You have the talents and the dreams – you just need to know where to begin and how to find the support to bridge the gap when you take your leap into your true being and purpose. That is where the L.E.A.P. into Your Dream Life begins.

Whether your leap takes you into a new career, entrepreneurship, relationship, or just establishing a new path that sings to your soul, this process will give you insights on letting go of that which is no longer serving you, evaluating your vision, assessing your skillset, and planning your landing to ensure that leap is a successful one.

The journey begins with taking those first steps from where you are now to where your new life begins, as well as the legacy you know you were meant to build for yourself and those who will follow you.

Join me on this L.E.A.P.!!!

Let Go of What Is No Longer Serving You

Have you ever asked yourself why you are holding onto an old shirt that doesn't fit anymore or is so threadbare it has outlived its purpose? Are you holding onto it for sentimental reasons, practical reasons, or because you were taught by others that throwing it away would be wasteful? Are you afraid to give it away because it is out of fashion and others may judge you for your wardrobe choices? Is that shirt your go-to comfort clothing?

You are probably wondering what questions about an old shirt have to do with leaping into a new life. So, let's reframe the questions: Have you ever asked yourself why you are holding onto an old job/position/career/relationship that doesn't fit anymore or that has outlived its purpose? Are you holding onto the job/position/career for sentimental reasons, practical reasons, or because you were taught by others that leaving would be considered wasteful on your part? Are you afraid to make a change because you will be considered out of your mind and others may judge you for your choices? Is that job/position/career/relationship your go-to comfort zone?

Just like letting go of that old shirt taking up space in the closet, you must let go of that which is no longer serving you in realizing your dreams, visions, and goals. By letting go of that old shirt, you are making room to explore new fashions and open up your wardrobe to new possibilities of color, pattern, and coordinate combinations. This is true when you let go of positions, places, and people who are no longer supporting your dreams, visions, and goals. When you open yourself up to new experiences, the possibilities for your future expand exponentially.

This process of letting go can be tricky, depending on how long you have been in your current situation. For some, the process can happen as quickly as deciding to let go and then letting go right then and there. For others, the process may take days, months, or even years. The latter of the two was my own experience, taking years to let go and learn to follow my own dreams and goals.

My interest in neuroscience and how the brain and body learn has led me to use techniques that have proven helpful in letting go of that which has no place in the life I know I am meant to lead. My interest in how socioeconomic status and emotional learning has led me to understand that mindset can have a direct correlation to a person's environment and relationships. I believe that mindset can be shifted to manifest the life of your dreams through the process of letting go of blockers and looking for accelerators toward the life you truly want to live. Mindset is where all transformation begins – where we set ourselves up for success to achieve our goals and dreams.

Evaluate Your Vision

Having a vision is important because it gives you a map and directions to travel from where you are now to where you want to be. Your vision will guide you each time you make a decision about the opportunities you encounter and where people fit into your overall plans.

Will the vision you create today be the same vision five, ten, or even fifteen years from now? Probably not! My vision has changed several times and will most definitely change several more times. Your vision will also be an ever-evolving plan that changes as you grow and change. Without a vision, you will be wandering through life living someone else's expectations and dreams as they guide you through a breadcrumb path of where they believe you should be. Work on creating your vision today – i.e. with a statement or vision board – then share that vision with your supporters.

Your vision will be the motivation to keep you moving toward your goals and dreams. When you put together all the pieces of your vision – business/career; finances; personal development; health and wellness; relationships; spiritual; location, and more – you will have the roadmap for the journey to the life of your dreams.

Assess Your Skillset

Our skillset changes as we learn and grow. We gain skills through experiences, training, and practice, but we also lose skills through lack of use and the aging process. Sometimes we only need a skill for a moment to complete a specific task and other skills we will need our entire lives.

If you took the ASVAB, ACT, or SAT during your school years, you may have been given a printout of some of your skills and the jobs or careers that may appeal to you and utilize those skills. You may have taken a skills assessment to determine your skillset. These types of questionnaires will help you plan for training or education to acquire or boost skills. What I find helpful to do with the questionnaires is to take the same assessment over time and compare how my skills have changed. It is interesting to see how the recommendations for jobs and careers shift as your skillset does.

Shifting your skillset can help you reach your dreams and goals through the acquisition of new knowledge, updated information, and honed techniques. Learning and growing personally and professionally will increase the opportunities available to you for careers, partnerships, and a host of possibilities in life.

Plan Your Landing

You have worked on your mindset by letting go of what is no longer serving you. You have let yourself dream about your future and evaluated your vision for your life. You have assessed your skillset to determine what skills you bring and what skills you will need others to bring to the table. Now you need to plan your exit strategy, next steps, and what your legacy will be for your family, community, and the world.

As you are planning your landing, you will need to keep in mind that as your foot touches down on the other side of the leap, you will be setting out on a new path.

Whether you come in for the landing at a smooth glide or arrive with a bang, you will have accomplished more than ninety-nine percent of the population ever attempt. New adventures, relationships, and opportunities await you on the other side. You are ready to take that leap.

The landing will set the foundation upon which you will continue the journey on a new path toward building your life and legacy. Let's get started with sticking the landing on the other side of the leap!

Keep Moving Forward

Remember each day to take the next step and keep moving forward. Be a better version of yourself today than the version you were yesterday. You are your only competition, and you have a cheering section and support system to help you reach your destination.

I took my own L.E.A.P. through this process of letting go of a career that no longer served my dreams. I wrote out a clear vision for my life, which I review and revise each year. Then I sought out opportunities to gain new skills, connections, mentors, coaches, and experiences that would guide me to the path on the other side of the leap and the beginning of a prosperous journey toward my future, the life of my dreams, and my legacy.

Stephanie Angle is the author of the best-selling book, *L.E.A.P. Into Your Legacy: Beginning to Build Your Dream* and an up-and-coming TV Producer on the Zondra TV Network. As an experienced speaker and presenter at virtual summits and live events, Stephanie has shared her message of transformation. In her work as a consultant and other leadership roles, she has demonstrated a history of being a change agent in the lives of those with whom she works. Her experience in the field of education has equipped her with special skillsets to work with individuals who want to experience transformation.

Stephanie Angle develops and facilitates sessions, workshops, and trainings built on neuroscience, mindset, and brain-based research practices. She guides her clients through a process to hone their content and deliver that content to maximize impact and engagement. Her strong leadership abilities, coupled with an educational course creation background, provide the basis for a well-equipped edutrainer who can move you forward in your personal growth and business goals.

linktr.ee/advantageangle

TRAVELING THE ROADS OF PROSPERITY

Indhu Athreya

Imagine that you are walking through a scenic route, one filled with beautiful trees, magnificent flowers, and pleasant fragrances. You taste the fresh air and feel the calming sea breeze. You have been along this route many times; it's your special place, filled with an abundance of luscious nature at every turn. Here, you can soak in peace and tranquility as you breathe in and let go of all of the tension and worry weighing you down, all the while feeling grateful towards nature for creating this realm of infinite bliss.

Now, how would it feel if you were always in this space? Imagine the things that you could create. How great would that be? This is how it looks and feels when you create something from a state of prosperity: a long-lasting marvel of joy and happiness. Prosperity is a state of being akin to the marvelous landscapes of nature. When you are in them, you feel a great sense of love, happiness, and gratitude; you create everlasting, impactful experiences.

I strongly believe you are here for a reason. You were guided to this book and this chapter for a reason. You may be here to browse and enjoy the reading, or to find some useful information. Or perhaps you're here to gain knowledge to create a transformation in your life. Regardless of your situation, you will be able to enjoy this experience because you truly are in a higher vibration – or beginning to align with that vibrational level – and ready to create magic.

To be in this state you have to create the proper climate. Imagine being able to feel cold in one-hundred-ten-degree weather. Living in Arizona, I know quite well that this is impossible. You need to be in a certain temperature to feel heat or cold. The same is true if you live in the desert and want to grow tropical flowers. The flowers won't thrive and bloom in that climate, so you must simulate the temperature controls and environment of the tropics. Prosperity is your true deepest self, as true as body temperature. When you are vibrating at this temperature, your energy field is filled with positive vibrations and only things that are in alignment with your levels will thrive. The question is, how do you get to this state, and sustain it, or what do you do when you get there? How can you create your dreams and desires from here?

Now, you may be wondering why you should believe what I have to say. Well, I am a transformational coach and hypnotherapist qualified in multiple alternate healing modalities, and I have been practicing and preaching these methods for over two decades. I have experienced firsthand the benefits and I have seen and listened to others who have benefitted as well. After facing many challenges, healing, and seeking knowledge from multiple gurus, my journey has taken me to a place of prosperity where I live in peace, awareness, happiness, and joy. From this space I was able to triple my income in a matter of months, surround myself with people who love and care about me, and open many doors of opportunities and abundance in my life. I am always grateful for all of it, and I always remain curious and stay present to see how it all comes into life.

Let us now dive into some actions for experiencing the magic of consciously and constantly creating and living the life of our dreams. These action steps are the ways I personally have used to gain success. Maybe many of you have heard similar ways and may have even practiced them. But the key is how you approach them, and how you follow them in your life every day.

1. **Intention**: The first step is to set your intention – clearly, with no ambiguity in there, and no wavering either. You must be *sure* about what you want, and trust without any doubt that it will all come true. For example, if you want a house, what type of house do you want? What type of community or environment do you want to be in? That said, you want to avoid getting into details such as the address, plot numbers, or how you want to get it. Intention-setting is not just the goal but the key. You are clearly conveying to the mind and the Universe your wish and your objective to achieve the same. Remember to stay realistic with your goals, as you need to trust that it is possible, and that you deserve to receive it. You will get what you want, but you have to first believe it to be true for you.

2. **Assessment**: Create an assessment of yourself specifically around the goal. What are your thoughts, beliefs, or experiences? How will you feel if you achieve this, and do you feel any resistance around this thought? Let's say, for example, that your idea is about staying healthy. Assess your past experiences, your conscious and unconscious beliefs, your successes, your failures, your blocks, your conditionings, your internal conflicts, your negative self-talks – everything that comes into your awareness about what is currently blocking you, as well as things that were successful but did not go as good as they could have. Write it all in your book of desires.

3. **Declutter**: Start decluttering your mind by using the inventory list you made in the earlier steps. Release all of them. If you find any resistance around releasing them, release the resistance first and then release the feelings. This step is like peeling an onion, the peeling keeps bringing in new awareness. Keep releasing

everything until you feel like there is no more to release. You can use any tool to release them like Hypnosis, NLP, guided visualization, violet flame, tapping or even simply saying, "I am ready to release, and I am consciously choosing to allow myself to release [insert the feeling, emotions, or anything from that list including events] and releasing all resistances." Remember, in all of this it's the thought that counts. Our mind stores every piece of information in its memory. Our behaviors, actions, and reactions to an incident is based on those memories. When you release them intentionally, you are rewiring your brain. It's like unlearning and learning something new.

4. **Design your desire:** Now that you have released everything you are like a clean slate, and in this clean slate you get to fill your intentions the way you wish them. First you start visualizing your happy place – a time when you felt utterly joyful, an event, or people that bring in these feelings within you. Stay in this feeling, or if you can, anchor this feeling and charge it often while meditating. Once you feel these feelings at their peak, now begin to imagine your desire. Visualize how it would look for you, feel for you, as if this has already happened. Again, we can create the desires only from the prosperity state of being. If you feel a lack of prosperity and still try to create your dreams, they will not come true, or the experiences won't be truly joyous, because your mind cannot hold two opposing ideas at the same time. If you believe that you will be poor, then you cannot dream to be rich. However, when you create from the state of prosperity, the results are in alignment. Create a daily ritual to visualize and feel it like it has already happened.

5. **Action your desire:** Apart from visualizing your dreams and desires in detail, start actioning by creating certain daily rituals. First create a journal – it can be a physical or a digital one – and

start writing in it daily. You may need one journal for your everyday experiences, another for Gratitude and Forgiveness, and yet another one for scripting with Gratitude as if all your desires have come true. Also remember that we are whole beings, so we need to feel, breathe, and live in prosperity to create the results of prosperity. This means eating the right food, like a healthy diet; treating yourself right; doing self-care; using only positive words; and thinking and doing positive rich things, all in alignment. If you feel any resistance or misalignment, go back to decluttering and release them. This is a process, and to stay prosperous you must continue to live this way every day.

6. **Be present and connected**: Stay connected with your inner self, the intuition, the higher source, or your unconscious mind. Watch for signs, stay open to receive, and do it with curiosity to see where it will take you. Remember to stay detached without expectations and remain inquisitive and act on those instincts.

7. **Celebrate**: Acknowledge that this is real work and give yourself credit for doing it. Celebrate even the smallest win. The win doesn't have to be the real goal; even the smallest hits are still wonders. The more you celebrate, the more results you will gain. Cherish them and feel the gratitude and continue to stay in this state to feel prosperous. Share and spread the joy.

We all want to create lasting happiness. Survival may be for the fittest, but life is for the living, so let's start right now. Raise your vibrations and expand your wealth, happiness, and joy. I sincerely thank and celebrate you all for being prosperous. Your vibration not only helps you, but also increases the abundance of lifestyle opportunities for those around you. You are changing the road map for them, and you are creating a beautiful place within and around you. You are on the road of prosperity.

Indhu Athreya is an IT professional, entrepreneur, transformational coach, certified hypnotherapist, NLP practitioner, mentor, and teacher. She has over two decades of experience in self-healing and has practiced and mastered over twenty different alternate healing modalities. Indhu holds an MBA and a certificate as an integrative healing arts practitioner from the Southwest Institute of Healing Arts (SWIHA) in Tempe, Arizona. She is very passionate about transformational coaching and empowering others in their conscious creation. Her motto is "Your inner wealth creates the external affluence." She brings her analytical knowledge and combines it with her spiritual wisdom to form a logical approach to her coaching and mentoring. Her hobbies include reading, painting, cooking, singing, and dancing, as well as puzzles and mysteries. Indhu lives in Arizona with her two children. To learn more about her coaching or to schedule your initial assessment call, please email her at:

team@sukhamindbodywellness.com

THE MYSTERY OF MONEY
Erin Christine

Shhh…listen closely…your body has something to say to you, something important that you're going to want to hear. She speaks a language you may or may not be familiar with, an electrical current rooted in frequency, vibration, and movement. But you must get still, stop where you are, close your eyes, and let your breath fill your belly long and slow, releasing even slower as you tune in to her whispers. Her wisdom is a deep buzz that runs in alignment with your energetic pathways, from the top of your head down to your toes, up and around again and again, never ceasing. The energy of All That Is lives within this vibrational current, including money.

What would you say if I told you that money is energy and nothing more? Does it trigger any sensation or emotion inside of you? If you think I'm nuts for saying this, good! This means there is healing to be done and we've just found a beautiful place to begin. The truth is, the mystery of money lives in your bones, its life force locked in each of your cells. Each one of us carries the vibrational imprint of our ancestors, the good, the bad, and the ugly. The energy of their struggles, their beliefs around money, and the choices they made all live within us. It's important to note that we all are doing the best we can with what we know in the moment. Think about the times your grandparents lived through, your great-grandparents, and what about their parents? Those were some dark, challenging periods, but they always wanted the best for their families and held their heads up in hope of a brighter future. Now I ask you to consider your own thoughts, beliefs, and behaviors with money. Are they truly your own, or are you operating from the imprint of your ancestors? We are going to explore that in this chapter and create a new energetic framework so you can embrace your personal prosperity and finally tap into the universal wealth that you so greatly deserve.

Energy is designed to move. When it gets stuck in our bodies, it creates stagnation and pain. The energy of money wants to move as well. As soon as we become aware of our relationship with money, we can begin to shift it to a more abundant, peaceful space. But we have to be willing to begin with our ancestral wounds around it. These are deeply-rooted wounds and the healing work requires commitment. It takes time to integrate the learning and move the energy and emotion through the body. We will touch on some simple ways to begin the process later, but first I want to talk a bit more about our ancestors.

They lived during a time when thoughts and beliefs around abundance were limited at best. Their bodies were hardwired for survival and the world as they knew it was only accessible based on what they could see. Hardships were plenty, and the only solution was to work harder. Fear was a daily visitor. Its presence took up residence in the bodies of each person it came into contact with. This fear became a natural, normal part of their everyday life.

One of the greatest gifts of spirit we all possess is the capacity to dream and envision a better life for ourselves, however, they could only expand their perspectives as far as their limiting beliefs would allow, which wasn't far at all. Also, each family passed along belief systems steeped in this fear to the next generation.

You, dear reader, are alive at a most auspicious and grand point in space and time. Never has there been more awareness, support, and resources available to expand the fire of consciousness within us all. This means that we have everything we need to move past the fears of our ancestors and create magical and prosperous lives for ourselves. The first step on this journey commands our awareness of what is holding us back. The following questions are designed to help you get thinking – or, better yet, feeling – what needs to be looked at to begin moving the energy of prosperity inside your body. When we can feel it, we can move it, and moving it allows us to make room for something better!

- Do you believe money to be the root of all evil? Why/why not?
- How do you feel about saving money?
- Do you resent others for having money? Why/why not?
- What stirs inside of you when bills come due each month?
- Do you feel you are worthy and deserving of having money? Why/why not?
- Do you feel you have to hide your money from others? Why/why not?
- Do you feel there's more than enough for everyone? Why/why not?
- How do you feel about sharing your money with others?

Let these questions be an exploration of your deepest self. Write freely, allowing whatever comes up to have its say. Be willing to surrender any judgments or criticism. This is a censor-free zone. When you feel complete in this exercise, close your eyes and take in a deep breath, you have just given yourself an important gift of prosperity. The willingness to look at our wounds is a brave first step on any healing journey, so be proud of yourself and take a moment to celebrate it.

The next part of this process can be tricky because it requires you to drop into your body and feel into the pain and discomfort that is attached to whatever came up for you as you journaled on the questions. This part will call for the utmost kindness and grace from yourself. Let's begin by calling in your ancestors to help guide your process. You'll want to make sure you're in a comfortable, quiet space where you won't be disturbed. The following prayer can be said silently or aloud to invite your ancestors to join you in your healing:

> *Wise and well ancestors, I call on you now to help guide me in healing any prosperity wounds that I may still have living inside my body. I am ready to release anything that is no longer serving my highest good. I give thanks to you all for the path you've walked, the challenges you've faced, and the courage it took for you to make all the decisions that made it possible for me to be here in this moment. Thank you for your bravery, your strength of spirit, and your perseverance, all gifts that I know live within me. I surrender to your wisdom, your grace, and allow the highest expression of your love to move through me now. Thank you. And so it is!*

Now that you've called in your ancestors, it's time to shine some more light on your wounds. Think back to the questions. Choose one and reflect on your response. Scan your body, starting at the top of your head, then move your attention down through your limbs, organs, and systems, noticing if and where any pain, tightness, or palpable sensations show up. When you feel a trigger, take in a deep breath, smile, and say thank you. Call the trigger by name if you know it, shame, guilt, resentment, et cetera, though it is not necessary to know what it is to successfully move the energy.

Then speak directly to it, saying, "Thank you, Shame. I see you and honor your presence here. I now choose to take back my power and release you so that I may receive that which I am worthy of. Release! Release! Release!"

Command it to release as many times as necessary until you feel the current begin to shift. As you speak to the energy, you may also choose to envision it moving out of your body. Assign it a shape and/or color and visualize yourself escorting it out of your body. Perhaps you're taking it to the trash can outside your home. You could even bundle it up into a big bubble and blow it back to the Universe. However you choose to release this energy is limited only by your imagination.

In the days that follow this process, you will be integrating your new awareness and allowing your body to settle into its new energy patterns. This can be an uncomfortable time. You may experience an influx of anger, sadness, grief, or any other emotion that is helping you move through this process. Let yourself feel whatever arises. Cry as much as you need to, scream if your body asks. You are moving generations of fear, it's going to take some time to settle inside your body. Memories may also surface, thoughts of loved ones passed or childhood reminiscence. This too, is part of the integration process. Remember, have kindness and grace for yourself at all times. You are doing the work your ancestors prayed for. They are so very proud of you!

Be sure to keep your journal handy as you move through the integration process. This is an exciting time for you personally, but also for your entire lineage! Pay attention to your words. You will begin to speak a new story. Your behaviors will change as well. You'll find yourself making choices that you would never have considered in the past. You'll now move through your days with bold confidence, even the rough ones, trusting yourself and knowing that your needs and desires are honored and taken care of by the loving, abundant source that gave you life.

Let today be the day that you decide to embrace the never-ending abundance of this world that is available for each one of us. Let this moment be the one when you choose to see yourself as the badass, magical creator that God intended you to be. Decide here and now that prosperity in all its glorious forms is yours to receive right now. Resolve to do the work to free yourself and your entire lineage from lifetimes of suffering and lack. Your new life awaits! Now go get it!

Faerypreneur **Erin Christine** is a tree-hugging, dirt-loving, bug whisperer who's constantly on the lookout for the greatest treehouse ever created to live out the rest of her days. She has experienced a curious, unusual life that has been fraught with sexual and emotional abuse, chronic pain, and unexplained health issues. She discovered the secrets to her healing could be found by connecting deeply with nature after being introduced to her spirit guides, the faeries, in 2002. This awakening has impacted Erin's life in marvelous, unimaginable ways.

Erin is a certified transformational life coach, licensed massage therapist specializing in reflexology/toe reading, and Reiki Master/Teacher. For two decades, she has traveled within and around the spirit realms navigating life as a clairvoyant, clairaudient, and empath. She uses the power of storytelling and elements of nature to empower the curious, playful woman to fully embody her unique voice and connect deeply to her spirit.

You can find Erin Christine frolicking among the trees in Fort Collins, Colorado, making friends with all the squirrels.

erinchristine.org

TENDING TO A PROSPEROUS SOUL

Melissa Kim Corter

The *soror mystica* ("mystic sister"), lives in every woman; she is an uncontainable force. It is impossible to extinguish her, for she is experienced as a channeled essence. She presents as a feminine archetypal expression of the alchemist – transforming beliefs about receiving, uncovering hidden desires and the ways by which we receive them. She appears as a deep aching of the heart, a relentless idea spinning in the mind, or an unrelenting hunger for something more. She is often ignored, abandoned, and betrayed… by the human self. And still, she persists and will not go away until unleashed. She understands prosperity, unhinging personal value from dollars or numbers in a bank account. She is not human, not really a "she," but more of an unyielding force that cannot be measured or contained – yet we constantly try to silence her presence. We numb out, disconnect, and soften her cries. We suppress her magic in order to fit into the world.

She mingles with nature, she lives in the elements, she is the allure of the flame, the whisper in the wind, the lusciousness of the earth, and the essence giving life to water. She is fierce and fluid, dedicated while detached; she holds no agenda yet can inspire action and reflection. She is the counterpart to the masculine, a sacred breath of creation, sexuality, and desire. We can work her magic to discover our own, she is a way-shower of truth and can lead you to prosperous aligned ways of tending to the soul.

Disenchanted

For many years I struggled to crack the code, trying to understand money, energy, thoughts, and the unconscious. I hired coaches and plunged into the everlasting wounds of traumatic events and memories all the while believing healing meant continuing to uncover and process... an unending cycle of never arriving and always needing to fix the wounded parts of me. Deciding I was no longer broken, and shifting awareness to the imaginal psyche, opened portals of possibility (and prosperity).

While pursuing my Ph.D. in Jungian archetypal studies, emersed in the psyche and shadow work, my calling evolved into furnishing my beliefs and actions with the magic I once felt as a child. To wonder is to be present, to be present is to allow the enchantment of life to speak to us – this is the language of the soul. As my life began to shift, my soul reclaimed the wonder I craved to feel. I began experiencing sacred encounters with the Universe, also known as synchronicities, discovering the hidden language of symbols embedded in the world around me. The Universe was leaving me breadcrumbs to find, little hints that everything was working out for me. It became my calling to acknowledge the medicine woman, the *soror mystica*, the wisdom-keeper and storyteller within me, and one who seeks to awaken in others.

Today, I walk women into the shadows, not to heal trauma, sit in pain, or find their wounds – but to retrieve the magic and re-enchant their lives and sacred callings. It felt miraculous to experience these divine surprises, as amplified levels of prosperity and abundance that arrived as a result of balancing the masculine and feminine. I allowed the hidden wisdom of the psyche to lead the way. In this chapter, I share a potent practice, one to awaken the *soror mystica* and attune you to the energy of prosperity with your desires and actions.

The Solution in the Symptom

Burning out four times in three years had a tremendous impact, and reflecting on this experience allowed me to see it as the result of a soul-sickness. Working with my psyche, Greek for the word "soul," lifted the veil clouding my vision and revealed the monotony of my day-to-day life. This sent me into a brief period of depression...until I encountered the archetypal forces contained in the symptoms. The burnout was an invitation to explore my psyche, to witness myself falling apart... a necessary breakdown of the "normal" for something greater to emerge. Burning out stirred the complacency settled in my bones; I felt like Sleeping Beauty suddenly awakening, a little disoriented and trying to find the ground beneath me. It took enormous effort to remain open and present to my soul, trusting it led me into a space of unlearning and detaching; I began to understand more clearly.

This is precisely when I began to understand the feminine essence, the *soror mystica,* and discover the ways I was denying her presence. Working hard, struggling, and hustling were strategies I lived by. None of them actually created success, they simply ensured I would have to work harder and prove my value and worth through effort instead of presence. The *soror mystica* was a different energy to embody; feminine in quality, there was a flow to her fire and a wisdom in her ways. Force was replaced with frequency and magic, and hard work shapeshifted into inspired actions – some of which included play, rest, fun, wonder, wandering, napping, and reflecting. The *soror mystica* delivered a sacred protocol, one I have shared with clients and use almost every day to make decisions in my private practice, teaching, and daily life.

The *soror mystica* invited me to cull the dead weight – figuratively and literally, with weight shedding as I arrived more deeply into my body, inhabiting this sacred vessel I had unknowingly abandoned over and over again. As my body moved through various changes, my soul asked more of me: more quiet, more stillness, more creativity, more fun, and more contemplation. Surprisingly, she also asked me to get comfortable saying the word no. My soul asked me to "sit with" requests instead of automatically saying yes; she revealed that these choices were delaying my desires. She asked me to trust more and fear less, to believe more and take risks… but the biggest ask was to let go of control. I had a love-hate relationship with her.

She broke down protective barriers and broke through the layers preventing me from owning my value and worth. Prosperity finally began reaching me and the more I trusted her, the more life reflected these changes. Instead of solving problems, I allowed myself to feel free of them – witnessing obstacles dissolve without needing to fix everything. This revealed a massive, sneaky, and hidden agenda: I harbored a deep fear of creating my life as I wanted to. Somewhere in the back of my mind were the horrid voices of my past, still trying to bully me. The *soror mystica* helped me release them, and hone my own voice.

Working Her Magic

If you feel called to work with the *soror mystica's* essence, the following two-part process will create the quiet and presence she requires to work her magic. Part one clears the space and ignites the senses. Part two aligns and attunes the feminine from a place of observation and inquiry. I also recommend using a journal to write down reflections and insights.

Part One:

- **Begin with intention.** Give yourself permission to be and feel whatever arises. Being close to nature helps to invoke her presence, so go to the beach, to water, mountains, the forest, or anywhere outside. Sitting by the light of the moon or in complete darkness (with a candle to see your journal) also enhances the experience.

- **What needs to go.** Write out a list of the habits, patterns, or experiences you witness yourself repeating. Pay particular attention to any masculine-dominated actions such as working hard, forcing, controlling, needing, or grasping behaviors.

- **What wants to stay.** Notice what works and serves you (not everything needs to go). What is coming together, what do you enjoy, what do you want more of?

- **What is ready to emerge.** Call in more flow, ease, grace, opportunities, money, wisdom, confidence, connection, rest, relaxation, and whatever your soul hungers for… Go deep with this, do not stay on the surface, playing it safe or focusing on what you can accomplish – the *soror mystica* is not a surface-level kind of presence.

Part Two:

The second part of this exercise involves wandering, wondering, and attuning to the inner fire and creative and prosperous power of the feminine. There are four questions I use to hone my energy when making decisions, creating new offerings for my business, and nurturing the magical elements of my life. I ask myself if the choice I am making passes through four energetic thresholds necessary for me to live a life of enchantment.

1. Is it *aligned?* Does this collaboration, decision, involvement, task, or endeavor align with my truth, authentic soul, and desire?

2. Is it *simple?* Does this situation, request, circumstance, desire, or interaction feel simple and have a sense of ease to it?

3. Is it *potent?* Does this experience, creation, and expenditure of energy feel like the most potent container for this experience?

4. Is it *prosperous?* Does the use of energy, time, money, or resources feel like a valued exchange based on my desires?

These questions are deeply encoded with the frequency of the feminine, a space for the *soror mystica* to speak on behalf of the soul. They are reflective mirrors offering the truth up to see from a different perspective, holding us accountable in a loving yet direct manner. The magic of the questions arises when you "work them" to support decisions and actions, asking the question before committing or following through. This provides an opportunity to readjust a response versus defaulting to old and disempowering ways.

Tending to Prosperity

As you may have gathered, money is not the sole expression of prosperity when viewed through a lens of enchantment; yet money certainly is not excluded and is quite welcomed! There are no limits or rules, yet there are desired states of being and feeling. Receiving is an art form to be cultivated and practiced; it might serve you to release any unconscious programming making it necessary for you to ask permission of others. This too is another magical representation of the *soror mystica;* she reminds you of your innate value – simply 'being' is your superpower.

Ease requires you to say no to the wrong things and yes to the right ones. "How" things work out is none of your concern – allowing and trusting are the keys. This is why tending to a prosperous life is a responsibility – a life of play, wonder, and curiosity. The rewards are plentiful and prosperity will never ask you to compromise yourself or another. Prosperous women are empowered and sovereign women. They give in accordance with what feels right, not out of obligation. They receive in a similar way: aligned, with integrity, knowing their value goes beyond dollars, and still money can flow and be accepted with gratitude and appreciation. Prosperity is one of the countless blessings of living an enchanted and aligned life. It is my hope that every woman tends to the sacred knowing within her. There is magic in your veins, and this world is desperate for your presence.

May the *soror mystica* be with you…

Melissa Kim Corter is a bestselling author, mentor, speaker, and teacher and is currently pursuing her Ph.D. in Depth Psychology and Jungian Archetypal Studies. Melissa believes in tending to the *soror mystica*, the inner feminine alchemist. This is the sacred pull, calling us to discover a deeper purpose and weave our authentic message into the tapestry of the world.

Melissa is a highly sought-after teacher and mentor, with accomplishments that include guiding thousands through practices and techniques during events with presenters such as Elizabeth Gilbert, Denise Linn, Dr. Joe Dispenza, Gregg Braden, Caroline Myss, and Martha Beck. She has been a guest on countless podcasts, and a contributor to numerous articles.

Her bestselling books include *Nudges from your Spirit*, The *Wild Woman* Series, and nine anthology books. In her home studio, Melissa loves creating wooden mandalas and curating sacred gifts that foster the re-enchantment of daily life.

When she isn't traveling or hosting retreats, Melissa is exploring the wooded and magical forests of Upstate New York with her husband, teenage son, and their precious fur baby Bella.

melissacorter.com

WHEN PROSPERITY CALLS, HOW WILL YOU ANSWER?

Vicki L. Dobbs

Yawning, I struggle to wake up. *What is that incessant noise?* I wonder to myself, rubbing the sleep from the corner of my eyes.

Hey, it's me! Answer the phone, blares an obnoxious, half-mechanical laughing voice. *Pick up, pick up, pick up. Hey, it's me, Prosperity! Answer the phone!*

Startled, I roll over and reach for the cell phone cradled on the nightstand, but there is no call to answer. The screen is black. Now I am awake.

What will you do when Prosperity calls? Will you answer? Are you ready to be prosperous and fly? Or are you still weighed down in scarcity mindset and lack? The best way you can increase your sense of "I am enough" is to change what you tell yourself.

Remember the old Indian tale of the two wolves that live inside each of us, one is good and the other bad? Think about this parable and consider for yourself, which voice do you listen to (feed), the "I am enough" or "I am not"?

If you believe that you can prosper, that you are prosperous beyond your bank account, then quite simply, you are. What does a prosperous life look like to you?

If you become what you think about, your life follows your thoughts like the saying, "As you think, so you are." To quote from an article by Sandy Gallagher, "You were born rich, and your abundance is contained in your thoughts."

Believe it and be it.

"But I can't," the voice wailed from somewhere off in the distance. "I can't, and I don't want to." I turned around, looking for the source of the sound and saw a father and son on the baseball field across the park. The little boy, wearing long pants that were too short, and a tattered blue and red T-shirt, crumpled to the ground as he tossed the bat he had propped on his skinny shoulder.

I strolled towards them and watched as the father tossed his baseball glove to the ground and walked off the pitcher's mound toward the little boy, his gait showing his obvious lack of patience. "You can," he demanded, "now get up and let's try again. If you don't' swing that bat a million times, you'll never hit the home run you're always talking about."

You could see the tears streaming down the little boy's face, pale streaks through the dirt now crusting his cheeks, as the tears turned dust into mud. "But Daddy, I never hit the ball," he sobbed, his little voice catching in his throat as he struggled to get the words out.

The dad, compassion now rounding his shoulders, scooped the little guy up, stood him on his feet and embraced him with both arms. Watching that hug brought tears to the corners of my own eyes. I walked a little closer being careful not to interrupt their process, but curious about how this little scene would play out.

The dad picked up the "kid-size" bat. It looked so short at the end of his long arms. "Here, son, you take this back." He held the little bat out to the boy's shaky hands. "Let's try this together." Seeing me across the field, the dad waved me over. Startled, I pointed at myself and he nodded an affirmation as I walked in their direction.

"Would you mind helping us?" the dad asked, picking up his own full-size bat off the ground behind them. "Would you kindly take that bucket of balls at the pitcher's mound and scatter them all over the ground, inside the bases here, in the infield?"

"Of course," I replied, scattering the balls about and then I moved myself behind the backstop, curious what the dad had in mind.

"Let's play whack a ball, son. You head towards first and I'll head towards third and we will whack all these balls back towards the mound. Want to?" he asked. "Watch," he called over his shoulder as he headed towards third holding the bat over his shoulder as though he were stepping up to home plate. Whoosh came the bat down off his shoulder as he swung with both hands and knocked the first ball across the infield.

"You try," he said as he turned back to his son. "Put that bat up just like I was going to pitch to you. When you get even with that first ball over there, use both hands like the great batter you are and swing away. Whack that ball across the pitcher's mound."

The little boy reluctantly started towards that first ball dragging his bat. He swung it from the ground at the first ball and missed. "Up on your shoulder, two hands," his dad called across the grass. The boy plopped the bat on his tiny shoulder, grabbing hold with his second hand; then, standing over the ball, he swung it more like a golf club than a baseball bat. Whack! He connected with the ball, and it rolled away, a tiny grin beginning to form in the corners of his mouth.

He strode off towards the next ball, his step a bit more confident, holding the bat with both hands just as if he were stepping up to the plate. Swing and a whack! Again the ball took off across the field.

I watched as he and his dad rounded the bases and smacked all the balls back to the center of the field, the boy now happily walking with a new sense of pride. "I did it!" he exclaimed as he and his father joined up at second base. "I hit them all."

"You set your eye on those balls and connected with every one of them," the dad explained as he knelt down to hug the little boy once again. "You found out you could, and you did!"

"Will you pitch a slow one to me, Dad? I think I can hit it now."

When you answer the call to Prosperity, one of the first things you learn is that with a "can-do" attitude, you can do and accomplish whatever you set your mind to. Your life will follow your thoughts just like the little boy discovered "he could" with the encouragement of his dad.

Follow these few simple steps and you too can develop a prosperous mind, body, heart, and soul:

Grow a prosperous mind. Live like a student, open to continuous learning, and pay attention to who you hang out with and listen to. Surround yourself with people who, like you, hunger for wisdom, knowledge, and success. Set worthwhile and worthy goals, as they are the roadmap to the life you want to live. Stretch your boundaries and grow consistently forward into the prosperous person you want to be.

Develop a sense of purpose. Know where you want to go and approach the path with your sacred intent and a determined focus. Drive prosperity with your divine purpose. Keep a prosperous mindset and prosper mindfully.

Live in a prosperous body. Your body is just as important as your mind when you determine you want to live a prosperous life. I don't mean that you will fit into the Barbie and Ken molds. What I am talking about is body movement and flow, strength and agility, ease and peace. A prosperous body is one that is nourished, comfortable, strong, and agile. The body you believe in and encourage will prosper with compassion, care, and love. Embody prosperity.

Share a prosperous heart. Be kind and kindness will be shown you, kindness is contagious. Remember the age-old saying, "As you give, so shall you receive?" Share all of you, not just from your wallet but from your heart. Share your words, your encouragement, propel another towards their dreams, and watch your dreams come true along the way. The return on your personal and emotional investments in others as in yourself, will exceed even your wildest imagination. Open your prosperous heart and prosper heartfully.

Maintain a prosperous soul with gratitude and prayer. Your gratitude, silently thought or spoken aloud, can change the energy you are living in almost instantly. Gratitude connects you with your Source, and paves the way for the good in everything, to move towards you. When you appreciate what's working for you in your life, practicing gratitude can actually boost prosperity in all areas of your life. Focusing on what is right in your world, what is working for you and what you are thankful for, will bring peace and ease to your days and open you to receiving prosperity into your life.

Be you, authentically:

- Believe you can and you will prosper.

- Embody your belief with your behavior instead of thinking one way while behaving another. Prosperity flows when you believe you are already prosperous.

- Embrace new wisdom and knowledge, engage in learning, and surround yourself with positive, prosperous people.

- Establish worthwhile and productive goals for prosperous living. Include the "f" words in your goal planning and make room for your faith, family, friends, finances, fitness, and fun.

- Practice generosity and kindness, gift everyone you meet with the best of you. Leave them feeling uplifted, supported, and encouraged when you part.

- Adopt gratitude as your go-to attitude. When you focus on the good in your life, the good becomes the focus of your prosperous life.

Be good to yourself, think good thoughts, build magnificent dreams, and never allow the physical world around you to control how you think. Choose you first, you have a right to be happy.

As founder of Wisdom Evolution and The You First Revolution, **Vicki L. Dobbs** has been helping people learn to navigate their lives in a way that allows them to gift the world with the best of themselves. She specializes in writing and crafting virtual and in-person courses that include some form of sacred creativity or art to anchor the teaching given into the participants' physical world.

Vicki is a Spiritual Entrepreneur co-creating with the Divine in opening existential gateways through which individuals can face their challenges as opportunities, embracing them as the revered teachers that they are. Using her best-selling books and courses, working with individuals, and speaking to groups, she endeavors to inspire others to create their lives intentionally. Introducing ancient wisdom techniques blended with modern modalities through experiential classes, ceremony, sacred art, and story, Vicki's goal is to see everyone live every day, empowered by the voice of their own authentic truth. She views this life's journey as an ever-upward, spiraling ascension of the human spirit leading it toward wisdom, wholeness, and joy.

vickidobbs.com

PROSPERITY IS IN THE LIGHT OF A WILD WOMAN

Lisa Eleni

I used to think that prosperity was associated with wealth. The more money I had, the more I could accumulate extraneous possessions. I wasn't necessarily a packrat, but I liked filling the nooks and crannies of my house with things I thought meant something to me or were a representation of my personality. I noticed that what I thought was valuable had shifted over time.

It wasn't until I was downsizing in preparation for a cross-country move that I began pondering the value of having all these belongings. I stood in my kitchen, surrounded by empty boxes to pack, and realized that a lot of my disposable income over the years had been used to accumulate more things so my house didn't feel so empty. I also realized they held a different energy for me now that I was starting a new chapter in my life. I wasn't as connected to the things as I once had been, but I was so overwhelmed with the move that it seemed easier to just pack everything and sort it out when I arrived in my new space.

As time went on, the weight of having so much stuff became somewhat obtrusive. I wound up having to move five times in two years and it was exhausting to haul all those boxes around and unpacking them, only to learn that I had to move again. The joy of having the prosperity to accumulate these items evaporated, and no matter how unique or beautiful they were, they no longer reflected who I was. They were merely holding a space that I no longer wanted filled from outside sources.

It was time to change my ideas about what prosperity really was. It was necessary to release my emotional hold on these items so I could make room for lighter, more relevant energy.

It occurred to me that I had come into the world with empty hands but a heart and soul filled with dreams, hopes, and legacies. Now, in order to fulfill them and have a positive impact on the world, I had to shine my light. Prosperity wasn't just about money and random things I acquired, but a myriad of other, intangible things that make up a lifetime: gratitude, celebration, living out loud, laughter, success, joy, fulfillment of dreams and goals, compassion and empathy. It was in sharing these priceless, unique gifts and leaving wonderful memories for those who were touched by my life that I could impact the world, not trinkets gathering dust on a shelf.

For the truly wild woman, prosperity comes in its purest form as light, that magical, magnetic light from within that draws people to you. Your inner light is your connection to a higher power. It generates in your soul and is manifested through your thoughts, actions, and words. Although there is simplicity in that mindset, it can be difficult, especially on some days, to maintain in a world that's not all unicorns and sparkles. Yet it is always available to you; you just need to take deliberate steps to keep it shining. That is how you become infinitely prosperous.

Surrounding yourself with like-minded and uplifting people can be an effective way of feeding your light. The people who lift you up are the tribe you want to surround yourself with, but you also want to be that light for them. In doing so you form connections, which is a form of prosperity.

Here are some other ideas of what to focus your energy on to replenish your reserves:

Meditation is your direct line to your higher energy source. It is the space in which we originated and to which we will return. Connecting to that energy source of unconditional love daily will help you eliminate distractions and concentrate on your path here on Earth. It is also a powerful tool for focusing your thoughts, which creates a prosperous mindset. Connecting each day for guidance, clarity, and soul-cleansing awareness recharges your inner light and makes it easier to see light in all areas of your life.

You must be mindful of your thoughts and release what is no longer for your highest good. Thoughts are powerful conductors of your inner light. Be a very careful wordsmith when you are engaging with your mind. Words have power, both negative and positive, especially when engaging in self-talk. Also, make your emotional health a priority and limit the intake of negativity in your environment – whether it is from people, the news cycle, or even fictional television shows you watch. This is particularly important if you are an empath like me, as your body can be a sponge for all that extraneous energy.

If you are feeling fatigued or suffering from pain, your body may be trying to alert you that you have reached capacity; make sure you are listening. One way to get the negative energy out of your body is to journal and burn. Write out your thoughts, fears, frustrations, annoyances, and any draining emotions from the people or situations that you are around. Once you are done, do not let it sit in your space! Rip those pages out immediately and burn them, rip them up or dilute them in water with the intention of releasing that energy from your body and transmuting it into energy for your highest good.

Releasing that negativity from your body will be cathartic. We all have triggers and stressors that we are doing our best to quell at any given moment throughout the day. They are actually here to be our teachers, so learn from them and delve into how they are happening for you, not to you. Get a new perspective and see the blessing, even in the discomfort, so these interactions are empowering and illuminating. Once you are in this place of discernment, you can shine your light and empower others to see the light in themselves.

Being in a place where you can hold space to support a friend's growth is a priceless form of prosperity. When you are in the light and can shine light on others to spark their own inner flame, it's magical for both of you. As you work through your heart space and share your light, you will impact those around you and exchange a wonderful, loving energy.

Another way to cleanse your energy is to get out in nature. The simplicity of planting herbs in a pot or taking a walk in your neighborhood to enjoy the scenery connects you to the most powerful source of life-giving energy there is. Even sitting on your deck and enjoying the sights and sounds of animals, wind, or rain can have rejuvenating effects on your psyche. It doesn't matter where you are – just step outside and take a moment to fill up those lungs with the amazingly fresh air; release that pent-up energy from sitting in on zoom meetings and negativity you are bombarded with, revitalizing your body, mind, and soul. This feeling will brighten your light and increase your emotional prosperity. It will also ground you and help you stay in the present moment.

Getting too far ahead of yourself causes anxiety and dwelling in the past keeps you mired in the should-haves and could-haves frame of mind. That said, some examination of the past can be beneficial. It takes you into the shadows, which are often a reflection of what you subconsciously reject within yourself. Shadows can also obscure wonderful things about you by filtering them through fear, shame, or doubt. Embracing your shadows can help free that unconscious side of you and allow you to step into your personal power so you can feed into light-giving pursuits without fear.

Your soul and body are unique to you. They are the core of your existence and need to be nurtured. Be kind to yourself; look in the mirror and tell yourself how much you love yourself, your talents, your beautiful body, and your amazing light. Let it be your go-to routine, rather than your quick criticisms of how you are somehow not whole or perfect. You are on the planet to have experiences, to learn and to bring your light to those you impact. You will feel more peace and joy and live a beautifully prosperous life that is spiritually fulfilling when you embrace all of your gifts and nurture yourself. Strive to be mindful of your thoughts and actions and connect to your light source. When you are connected to your highest power, you are a reflection of amazing light. You understand that prosperity comes in the form of joy, comfort, creativity, nurturing, and security of being your most authentic, loving self, and that your light comes, not from a store, but from within.

Lisa Eleni is a spiritual artist, healer, intuitive tree reader and Mind-Body-Spirit practitioner who resides in Colorado. She is also the founder of Healing with Heart, which focuses on empowering women by creating a safe space for individual healing and reflection using meditation, art, and journaling. Lisa creatively incorporates art activities to hold space for like-minded people to befriend and support each other each month in her intentional woman's artshops. Her passion is encouraging women who desire more joy-filled, authentic lives with intention.

Lisa is also an author, with published work that includes chapters in Sunny Dawn Johnston's *Prayers and Meditations* and Melissa Kim Corter's *Wild Woman's Book of Shadows* – both of which are Amazon bestsellers. For more inspiration and the latest information on artshops and new publications, visit:

lisa@lisaeleni.com

MY DANCE WITH PROSPERITY

Rachel Elizabeth

When approached by Melissa Kim Corter to write a chapter for this book, I was shocked. I mean, me? Prosperity? Seriously? How could those two things even be in the same sentence? Let us just say at the time I wasn't feeling very "prosperous." The bills were piling up and the bank account was getting lower and lower. You see, like many others I had decided during the pandemic to prioritize what I really wanted and go for it. That meant giving up my longtime career as a bartender and server extraordinaire to step into my destiny as an intuitive jewelry designer specializing in the Tree of Life. I started my business the following year, and though I knew I was going to make it, at the time, well, things were looking kind of dim.

Then it then dawned on me that Melissa was not asking me to write in this book because of any number in the bank account, but the prosperous way of being I had embodied during this unique and monumental time. After all, the last four years have been the most transformational in my life, not just in terms of my career, but my entire existence.

Quarantine

As I write these words, I realize that it is the fourth anniversary of my mother's celebration of life. She had passed away on March 29, 2018, ten days after my thirty-ninth birthday, from complications of a blood clot. So while my birthday at the start of the pandemic in 2020 certainly wasn't the greatest, it was nowhere near as bad as the one I'd spent holding vigil at my mother's side for all those hours.

It was in those weeks when we were all collectively "sent to our rooms" that I truly started to embody my prosperous life. My life partner Steve, who was self-employed as a carpenter, continued to work and we were incredibly lucky for that. But on those long days when he was at work and I was drinking wine for breakfast (I mean seriously guys, what is happening right now? Is the world ending?), I was in and out of the collective fear. At the same time, I was reintroduced to spirituality, and it could not have come at a better time. That is when the real work started.

Connection

How prosperous were we all to have the internet during the pandemic? Though we were physically disconnected, we were able to Zoom and FaceTime each other and still be in constant contact. I was so blessed to find so many talented writers, speakers, changemakers, and mentors – most of them in the spiritual industry. With all these classes, seminars, books, and livestreams all at my fingertips, I felt as if I had won the lottery!

It was then that I started my daily meditation practices, journaling programs, and other gratitude practice for everything that truly was positive in my life, including Steven and our three cats. We were fortunate, dare I even say prosperous?

Hiking

For me, another form of prosperity – and the most impactful – is nature. I have a deep connection to the trees, and the magic and wisdom of these stunning beauties resound deep within my soul. The ancient stories they hold and the years of natural provisions they provide is astounding.

The pandemic made me an avid hiker, as it was amongst the trees in the hills and the trails of Connecticut and greater New England that I felt the closest to my crossed-over loved ones and with Spirit. Before my maternal grandmother, Lillian, passed away, I had asked her what signs she would send me when she transitioned to the other side. Her response was, "Trees." When I asked how she would send me trees, she replied, "You will see." She then drew a tree on a piece of paper in front of me – a tribute to the artist she was.

It wasn't until the morning of her passing on January 6, 2021 that I remembered this conversation. I had already started to create Tree of Life wire-wrapped, crystal cabochon pendants, and I realized that though she had never gotten to see one in person, she had sent me the inspiration – a true gift of prosperity from beyond the veil. It would become what my entire business is based upon. To this day, while hiking in the woods for inspiration, I am reminded to set aside my mind and ego and let spirit gear me through to the hardest part. That's when you know the difference between mind body and spirit, because at the very end it's your spirit that gets you to the last leg. Like all things we do in life.

Sisterhood

The last half of 2021 was a doozy: my mother's brother passed away suddenly, Steven suffered a mild heart attack, and then his father had a massive stroke and passed away sixteen days before Christmas.

I mean, how does one even begin to feel any sense of prosperity under these circumstances?

I was feeling completely down as I continued to navigate life and all its twists and turns. Then, on the Saturday before Christmas, I got a phone call that changed my life and restored my faith. My friend and mentor Sunny Dawn Johnston called to tell me that someone had paid for my healing retreat in Sedona, Arizona! I felt immediately blessed and undeniably grateful for the generosity of this anonymous donor. (She is also a fellow author in this book whom I love dearly.)

I continued to experience this generosity during my trip to Arizona. Women I had met only over the internet opened their homes for me to stay; they paid for garden tours, and lunches. I was even able to stay an extra week at a beautiful golf resort! Prosperity showed up in ways I could never have imagined. I am still grateful for that experience to show me what is still possible, even in the depths of great despair. As for Sedona itself, it is a magical place, and I could write an entire book just on my time there!

The Open Road

Last year, my man fell back in love with Harley-Davidsons and purchased one without consulting me first, knowing darn well that I would have objected. I quickly moved into the energy of acceptance, because I knew I needed to get over my fear and other people's perceptions of how dangerous motorcycles are. What does that have to do with prosperity, you may ask? There is an incredible sense of prosperity on the other side of fear. The thrill of the open road ignites your senses and really pulls you into present moment awareness. There are smells, sounds, and sights that you can only get from the experience of riding. It's the dips in the temperature when you are up and down the beautiful hillside. It's the smell of the fresh-cut grass as you zoom by the neighborhoods' homes early on a Saturday morning. It is the closest thing to flying I can imagine. When you decide to move past the other side of fear you get a feeling of prosperity that reminds you are here, alive, if only in this very moment. I have learned to love the motorcycle and riding it is one of my favorite things to do. The neighbors think I'm a little bit crazy when I'm outside calling on Archangel Michael for divine protection and doing a sage ceremony on our bike before we take a ride. And I am okay with that.

Mountains and Music

One of my favorite places in the world is Vermont, with its lush green mountains and crystal-clear rivers and farmlands reminiscent of yesteryear. If prosperity was an actual state, this would be it. Admittedly, I'm a little biased because my grandparents were born and raised in Thetford, Vermont, a small town near White River junction. There were three sisters in my grandmother's family – the "Young girls" – and three "Palmer boys" in my grandfathers'. All the Young sisters married the Palmer brothers, a tribute to small-town life back then. I often think about what that life must have looked like, and I am lucky to visit that small town occasionally. Though my family is gone, the memories are still there.

In Vermont there is a small town called Stockbridge. My good friends Heather and Rick are super talented musicians and have created a prosperous life there through their art of music, food, laughter, luv, and connection. The Wild Fern is a magical little roadside cafe that has a cigar brunch every Sunday, with fresh bagels and a jam session. Any time you are lucky enough to have talented musicians come together, there is an embodiment of prosperity, whether it is in large-scale concerts, sold-out arenas, or even a small drum circle in your local quarry. Music brings people of all walks of life together, each of there for all different reasons but for the same purpose. To me, that is a feeling of prosperity like no other.

Simplicity

Of everything I have learned in these last four years of deep grief and self-exploration, the biggest takeaway is that real prosperity lies in your relationships, your everyday habits, and your true connection to Source.

Prosperity is the simple things: a walk-in nature, a lovely home cooked meal, music that moves you in the quiet stillness of the morning. Prosperity is how you view the world even when it is handed you a bunch of lemons and you have little in the bank account. Prosperity is all around you, you just must look for it. Prosperity is not a destination; it is a feeling, a sincere desire to embody prosperity it in all that we do. After all, prosperity goes hand in hand with gratitude. If you will allow yourself to feel immense gratitude, then prosperity will show up in diverse ways and all the time. Sometimes in miraculous and unexpected ways.

Rachel Elizabeth is an intuitive jewelry designer and artist who incorporates the healing modalities of the Tree of Life into her work. Rachel loves all things mystical and magical and is constantly continuing her education in all things concerning science, spirituality, and art. She is a crystal enthusiast and is currently studying lithotherapy, stone healing. Recently, Rachel Elizabeth became a mind, body, spirit practitioner studying under Sunny Dawn Johnston; she also studies under Melissa Kim Corter and is fascinated with the Jung Archetypes. Rachel Elizabeth runs the wildly popular Facebook group, "Creativity with Rachel Elizabeth Design." When she is not creating beautiful pendants, you will find her out in nature. Rachel Elizabeth lives in Central Connecticut with her life partner Steve and their three cats, Berrie, Luscious, and Myles.

rachelelizabethdesign.com

QUICKSAND

Sandy Hanshaw

One of my favorite things to do as a child was watching Saturday morning cartoons, especially Scooby Doo. I vividly remember sitting cross-legged as close to the tv as I could and still see the screen. They were always chasing a "ghost" and finding themselves in some sort of distress, and then the big reveal showed the bad guy was someone who'd been in their face the whole time. Based on the show, I thought I would run into quicksand around every corner, and a sense that has been true – not in my physical world, but in my mind and mindset.

Well into my teens I often made decisions based on the excitement factor rather than potential consequences. I have had some interesting "adventures" and often wonder how I made it out of some of them. What I didn't realize was that I was manifesting those adventures because I was confident in what I wanted and the Universe delivered them to me. The mindset I had was creating the life I wanted. I am going to share some inspiration on how shifting your mindset can totally change your life. Sounds easy enough, right?

Our thoughts are the most powerful tool the Universe has given us, well that and the fact that we are all amazing individuals with our own special unique talents. We are our own best manifester of greatness and have the power to create our own best reality. We can also manifest an absolute shitshow for ourselves if we don't mind our thoughts. From early on in life we are taught to think, act, and do what others tell us so we can fit in and make it easier for authority figures to remain in control. In the process we end up losing our imagination, creativity, and the qualities that make us so special.

Every morning when we wake up, before our feet even hit the floor, we have the opportunity to make the first decision of our day, and that is what kind of day it will be. In that moment, take a deep breath in through your nose and out through your mouth. Tell yourself you are going to have a fantastic day and you are happy and grateful for it. Doing this one thing every morning will not only change the way your day starts, it will positively affect your entire day. In fact, and you will soon start to notice how many great days you are having.

The moment we start believing what is not seen, our entire reality will shift. Think about it, when you keep reminding yourself you are having a bad day, doesn't the bad day just keep coming at you? Why not shift your thinking about what an amazing day you are having? Ever been thinking about buying a certain kind of car and then – bam! – that car is literally *everywhere?* They have always been there; the difference is your thoughts are now focused and you are bringing those thoughts into your reality. We must believe we are going to have what we desire before the validation of manifestation magic shows up. We have become a society of "show me first and then I will believe." This is totally backward when it comes to manifesting our desired reality.

I want to share an example of a recent personal manifestation. I had been wanting to go on a spiritual retreat but couldn't find one that worked with my schedule. I decided in January of 2022 that I would block out every weekend in the month of June and manifest the perfect retreat for me. Keep in mind, I did not do any research or have anything in mind when I set this intention. I only had a desire to meet likeminded people in the month of June. In preparation for this to happen, I updated my personal and work calendars to show I was unavailable for every weekend in June – and that I was at a retreat. I also started saving money, purchased a new outfit to wear, and started to journal how amazing this retreat was going to be. I believed wholeheartedly and felt it to my core, this retreat was going to be life-changing for me and I was going to meet new women to add to my tribe of soul sisters.

On March 7, 2022, I saw an ad on social media about a spiritual retreat the first weekend of June – and it was within driving distance of my house! I had already saved the money needed, and it was with someone I have wanted to meet and work with for the past several years. The Universe had delivered above and beyond what I asked for. It had given me an extra scoop of awesome for my efforts.

Mindset is the game-changer on attracting abundance and prosperity. I view abundance and prosperity as joy, health, happiness, healthy relationships, finding your tribe, and financial wealth. All of this means something different to us individually, so it is important to define what abundance and prosperity is to you, and then release judgement on others. Remember, you don't know their story or what it means to them.

I want to dig a little deeper here and provide another example of how our way of thinking changes the trajectory of our lives. A program is offered with a $2,500 tuition fee and there are fifteen attendees. Everyone is given the exact same course materials, same resources and, on the last day, the same pep talk from the facilitator. Every person in the program wants to succeed.

One person from the group is now earning six figures and the remaining fourteen people are signing up for another program because they are convinced the one they just took didn't work. The difference is that one person wholeheartedly believed in themselves and worked the program. There was no doubt in their mind; they were confident in themselves and knew they were going to succeed. The remaining fourteen, though they had the same exact information, did not achieve their goals because they doubted themselves and didn't put in the work. And guess what? The next program they sign up for will not work either if they don't change their mindset.

You have to put in the work, follow the process, believe unequivocally in yourself and all of your dreams, and more will come rolling into your present. It can be scary, and this is usually where we talk ourselves out of the best idea ever, but remember, the other side of fear is FREEDOM!

Our thoughts and beliefs become our reality. The Universe does not know the difference between what we are thinking and physically doing. We all have that friend who always puts themselves down somehow: "I suck at relationships"; "I can't parallel park"; "I never get the promotion"; and so on. When saying things like this to yourself, you are affirming to the Universe that is what you desire. Personally, I wish I would have known this tidbit earlier in life so I could have parallel parked for my driving test because I wholeheartedly convinced myself it could not be done and, in that moment, it couldn't! Failed It!

Start to pay attention to your friends who are living their best life. Do you ever hear them speak negatively about themselves or their lives? Someone tells them they look nice and they say thank you – they don't respond with comments about not doing their hair, wearing old clothes, or something else negative. They do not make excuses for their greatness. We are emotional beings, and while it is important to feel through all our emotions, it is equally as important to not dwell in the negative emotions and create a cozy place there. Give yourself a time limit to go and have your pity party and then, when the time is up, move on to the next wonderful thing in your life. I have found challenging situations in life are not punitive, but the Universe's way of trying to teach me a lesson. Changing my mindset to look for the lesson rather than feeling punished has immensely changed my life for the better.

One of the simplest yet most challenging things to do is figure out what you really want. It is important to get clear about what you want and narrow it down to get more of it in your life. Again, the Universe does not know the difference between "good" and "bad," so mind your thoughts and bring in the awesomeness you want in your life. Where you put the thoughts and energy determines what will come forward. It is not enough to say, "I want a promotion." You need to define the attributes of the position, for example, "I want to be the Director of the Department. This position will allow me an office with a view, access to the good bathroom, facilitate classes, get a better apartment, buy a new car, take better vacations, etc." Now that you clarified what you want you can ask for it and start calling it into your reality.

Yes, you will have to do more than just ask, but it doesn't feel like work when you have a passion for it. Take steps to prepare yourself for the role. Do you need to learn a new computer software, share innovative ideas, and find ways to meet the right people you would need to know for the position? If the answer is yes, then start doing those things now. Stay open to all opportunities and release judgement of what they should look like.

Vision boards are a great tool to help manifest your desires as well. Let's stay with the example above of getting a promotion. Create a vision board for the promotion and the opportunities that come with it. What does your new office look like? What type of clothes will you wear? How many people will you lead? You get the point – put the desire and energy into the board and then keep looking at it and feeling it. This is the step most people don't follow through on with vision boards. You can't just make it and walk away; you have to keep putting the passion, desire, and energy into bringing it to fruition.

My final thoughts…

Scooby was right, and quicksand is everywhere! Approach life from a place of abundance and prosperity. Believe it is possible, know it is available, know you deserve to have it, do it, and be it. Give yourself permission to be you regardless of what others think and say. The Universe is waiting to give you all you want!

Sandy Hanshaw is a bestselling author, Intuitive Soul Coach, Reiki Master Teacher, and Integrative Healing Arts Practitioner. She is passionate about assisting others in finding their purpose and truth through education and self-discovery, while using her unique combination of humor and intuitive gifts to provide practical guidance. Sandy holds a Bachelors of Metaphysical Science and is currently pursuing her doctorate in Metaphysical Counseling.

She has over twenty-five certifications, including Usui Reiki Master/Teacher, Transpersonal Life Coach, Mindfulness Guided Imagery and Meditation Facilitator, and Certified Belief Clearing Practitioner. She offers her gifts as an intuitive, to clear and balance stagnant energy while empowering clients to find the best version of themselves.

Sandy loves to travel to new places, meet new people, and has created a line of spiritually-infused products. She loves a good girls' weekend which might include anything from wine-tasting and train rides to paranormal investigations. She lives in Oak Ridge, Tennessee with her husband and fur babies.

sandyhanshaw.com

SPIRITUAL SALT AND PEPPER PROSPERITY

Maribel "Belle" Hernandez

Can you imagine winning the lottery? Imagine yourself one year after winning. What does your life look like? What fears pop up? If you are like most people, you are worried about losing family, friends, or all of your money. Perhaps you have heard that most people who win the lottery end up filing bankruptcy.

Now, can you imagine maximizing the money, time, and energy you have right now and always having more? Can you imagine feeling so good in your own body and all aspects of life that you are excited and happy to be alive? Waking every day with a zest for life, giving the first few minutes of your morning to Source, and connecting to your own truths? It is possible that through consistent practice you will be able to build a strong spiritual foundation and the ability to sustain what life throws at you – especially large sums of money, happiness, and health.

For several years now I have been the Owner of Agape in Action and a spiritual coach and mentor. Agape in Action is my personal love project, my way to connect people to the tools they need to consciously create their lives – and feel worthy of the miracles they manifest. I meet people where they are in their lives and support them in connecting to any shadow aspects that are holding them back. By embracing the shadow and diving deep for the gold that the shadow contains, clients are able to overcome fears and limiting beliefs around prosperity. Using these tools, I have helped hundreds of women and men over the years; I have also used them to create a life I love.

Here is the path that brought me to what I call the "Salt and Pepper Principles." The year 2014 was one of immense stress and loss. My beloved dog died, my long-term relationship ended, and I was depressed, anxious and unsure whether I would be able to survive financially. Looking back, this was a limiting belief – I was well-paid and fully able to thrive. I had so many other limiting beliefs as well.

Spiritual Salt: a friend took me to yoga and my journey began! The breath work at the beginning of the practice connected me to my body, the movement freed my body of the constrictions of stress, and the meditation connected me to the bliss of my spirit. This alchemical process was freeing me from a lifetime of restricted energy and trauma, one class at a time. I was hooked and began practicing yoga daily. I meditated, spending at least thirty minutes a day connecting. I practiced yoga nidra multiple times a week to keep my peace. I added hypnotherapy as well to access different aspects of the sub-conscious mind. I prayed my mala, with the mantras changing as I broke mala after mala and completed the cycle of what I prayed to be connected to. By praying the Gayatri Mantra, I grew strong in my discernment.

I also journaled around my breakthroughs or obstacles. Some days I would sit and think of the things I was grateful for and write them down. Page after page, a history of my obstacles, opportunities, and evolution. I focused on cultivating the energy of joy and gratitude daily. Every morning before my feet hit the floor I would say, "I wake today with joy and gratitude" – a mantra suggested by my mentor at the time. She told me that one day I would feel it, and she was right! I was grateful for the little things, from watching the sun rise and set to puppy kisses and the taste of chocolate. I created a pie chart of things that brought me joy and colored it in as I consciously chose to do those things.

In the spring of 2015, a friend offered me a trip to Hawaii while I was in-between abundances, awaiting a tax return. I came home that night, sat in my meditation chair, breathed, connected, and said out loud to Spirit," Alright guys, if I am to have this trip, expedite my tax return." I let go of the outcome and went to bed. It was in my bank account the next morning – weeks before it was due to arrive! I hopped into my meditation chair filled with joy and gave gratitude for the blessing.

Spiritual Pepper: I dove deep into shadow work, I wanted to know what was running my life if I hadn't been. I dug deep into the shadow of "Angry Annie," she was trying to protect me from taking the wrong actions and I suppressed my anger. Annie and I talked and she agreed to connect me with the right actions at the right times and I learned healthy ways to process anger.

I got crystal clear about what kind of prosperity I wanted to manifest. Did I desire joy, love, money, and so on? I got crystal clear and thanked the Universe when it came. Each time, I imagined who I would have to become to align with what I wanted to manifest. Who was this woman? How does she dress? How does she feel about life? What does she eat for breakfast, lunch, and dinner? I had to get ready for my rebirth as her.

Once I dreamt up this woman I was becoming, I looked at limiting beliefs and stories that were holding me back. How could I rewrite these stories? Who would I get to be without them? I realized this woman I was becoming needed me to love her deeply. I started to ask myself, What is the most loving thing I can do for myself in this moment? I doubled down on my self-care, exercised daily, went to the float spa, got my hair done, ate good food, listened to good music, and spent time with people who loved me. I set goals for myself and broke them down into daily action items. Each day I would do one small thing (I call them "small bites") toward my goals. For example, if I wanted love, I would plant love at home by being present and loving to my pets, friends and family. And then the world by sharing a kind word or a smile with a stranger.

I looked at where I was putting my energy, and if it didn't serve my highest good I made changes, bringing my focus back to my goals, my wants, my needs, my desires, self-love and community connection.

I started to clear out what no longer served me. I got rid of clothes that didn't express who I was inside. I moved yearly, and with each move was a new opportunity to clear out old personal items. I also cleared out the old energy and thought patterns. I filled in the spaces with my dogs, people, and items that sparked joy and that I loved. I filled in any empty spaces with love, making sure to leave some room for creation.

Opportunities flowed to me as I grew my spiritual fortitude. New clients were connected to me through current clients, friends, and classmates. The more I healed myself and connected to my spiritual prosperity, the more clients showed up.

I used the Spiritual Pepper and worked on healing any and all aspects of my mind, body and Spirit that needed it. I put myself as my top priority and loved me the most. I asked myself what brought me joy and did that. I added integral breath to my morning meditative process, as well as other techniques I learned in my yoga therapy program and watched as my experience of life became one of immense peace and joy.

One day I woke up and realized that I had become the woman who lived the life I dreamt for myself. The tools in the Spiritual Salt and Pepper principles had given me my mind, body, and Spirit back. I have also witnessed others being carried by Source energy and provided for because they applied these principles.

To practice Spiritual Salt and Pepper, set up a sacred space where you can meditate and connect to your prosperity. Your sacred space can be in nature near your home or work where you feel safe, grounded, and connected to Source. Bring with you items that connect you to Source, like crystals, pictures of loved ones, or spiritual books/items.

Your sacred space does not have to be large. Mine have been of various sizes, including a den, then a meditation chair, then a den again. Oftentimes, I would set up sacred space in my car! I also have a sacred space out in nature that I will hike to when the weather is nice. My guru and many spiritual teachers visit me while I'm in meditation at this location. Connection and consistency are key; find what works for you and the space that you have, and do that.

Spiritual Salt

Spiritual Salt is flow that allows the energy to move through barriers. These practices move the energy you have available for manifesting prosperity of any kind. These practices can be done daily, all together or in any combination.

1. Breath – start by witnessing.

2. Meditate – nidra/hypnotherapy.

3. Move – I recommend yoga.

4. Shadow work – Look at the aspects of your life that you avoid; these are gold.

5. Prayer – I suggest using a mala and a mantra.

6. Journal your experiences, emotions, and dreams.

7. Cultivate joy and gratitude.

Spiritual Pepper

Spiritual Pepper is the fire; the action, the alchemical aspect of preparing for prosperity, of transforming scarcity into worthiness. These practices are to be used as needed or, dare I say, "to taste."

1. What kind of prosperity do you want to obtain (joy, love, money, et cetera)? Get crystal clear.

2. Who are you willing to become to obtain what you want? Map out every detail of the life of this person you will become. Start doing what they do.

3. Identify limiting beliefs you are willing to change; change them to be empowered.

4. Love yourself, first and the most!

5. Take one small step each day towards your goal.

6. Keep your focus on what serves your highest good.

7. Clear out what no longer serves you. Fill in this space with lots of love.

Consistent practice of these principles supports my embodied alignment with the universal stream of well-being and keeps me present and joyful, able to receive all prosperity that comes my way. May you too live your life embodied, able to receive all prosperity you desire. May your spirit be victorious, Jai Bhagwan.

Maribel "Belle" Hernandez is a Reiki Master Teacher, Intuitive, spiritual life coach, hypnotherapist, integral breath therapist, yoga nidra facilitator, yoga teacher, and dog mom. In 2014, after years in a high-stress career, Belle was pushed to her limits. After being invited by a friend Belle went to a yoga class and was immediately hooked. Yoga helped Belle radically transform her life, and fueled her passion to guide others on their journey to peace and transformation. In 2016 she founded Agape in Action, a spiritual coaching and wellness practice to connect clients with the tools needed to overcome trauma and barriers so they can consciously create their lives. She is increasing her community reach year, after year, working one-on-one with clients and holding group classes and workshops.

Belle is currently on the path to graduating from the Amrit Yoga Institute in December 2022 with her Yoga Therapy Certification.

You can usually find Belle with her pups Archer, and Louise. When the weather is cool they are out hiking the Phoenix Trails.

agapeinactionaz.com

SOULFULLY ABUNDANT

Patricia Horton

You are each born abundant in nature, and with a free flow of energy at your fingertips to use as you choose. The duality of the physical and the spiritual is your birthright, as you were born on the wave of feminine (mother) and masculine (father) energy.

Today I want to share with you the spiritual aspect of this mother/father energy – a teachable moment from my own understanding. Creation is but a thought away, as a world of opportunity is waiting to be accessed by you. It is throughout the Universal Mother's playground (feminine) that you create within, through the spark of God's Divine Light (masculine) of creation within you. This is where the duality of creation is empowered and utilized.

When I speak of the "Universal Mother," I am connecting you to the unfertilized egg of feminine energy – from which all things are created. When I speak about "God's Divine Light," this is where the egg is fertilized by the masculine. You each have your own part to play as you dance underneath the umbrella of both aspects. Your part is to engage your imagination to gain access to both. This is where you will begin to visualize your desire for the tangible that creates your reality. Now is when I will ask you to allow your imagination a playground to explore within, as we connect the dots.

As the child within you reaches, know that you are supported by the Universal Mother and allowed to stretch as far as need be without being coddled. You see, a loving Mother will always be the support system in which growth is encouraged, and where Mom's strength, love, and guidance becomes her gift to the curious child. This is where she will allow the child to fall when need be, as she views growth as a learning process. She knows from experience that it is the curiosity of the child that sparks the imagination, and from this point forward, manifestation of all things occur. This is where Mom provides a safe space within The Universal Mother's arms to awaken the sleeping child within you. This Universal Mother holds your spiritual hand as you walk through the living world. She becomes the teacher who provides opportunities for growth. She understands the soul's yearning for learning, and like an intuitive parent, she guides you. The Universal Mother helps you to create all things, and she lends her support to your creative endeavors. This is where the spiritual side of life becomes intertwined with the tangible world, creating from a place of knowing within you.

The Universal Mother will set a place for you at her table, to sit and eat from as you nourish your individual soul's growth. It is by choice that you find your way to the bounty offered. It is through your own free will, and under her guidance, that you will actively engage with your abundant nature. As you sit at her table, take a look around you. See how you are surrounded by your brothers, and sisters in spirit as she gently guides all of you with love and kindness. She loves all of her children equally and shows no favoritism. This is where an understanding is gained by you, that you are each blessed with the opportunity to learn equally while here.

Now, to create something tangible the feminine energy needs the masculine to fertilize the seeds planted within her womb. This is where "God's Divine Spark" comes into play. To fully understand your abundant nature, you will need to have an understanding of the masculine aspect as well.

God is the masculine counterpart who works in concert with the Universal Mother and you. The act of creation becomes a beautiful solo waiting for the orchestra to join in, and where the composition of the piece being played can be appreciated and enjoyed. In simple terms, it is the divine hand of God that supports, nurtures, and loves all things that are created within the mighty Universe, which, without God, would be void of this love. God's love harnesses its own musical tone, and it is within this loving vibration that you were each created equally. The Mother's womb is fertilized by the Father's seed, through God's Divine Spark of love for you. It is through the power of creation within the Universe that this was made possible.

As you extend your hands outward, you touch the world and all within it, and where He can be felt by everyone, when you do things from the heart center. This is where you become the example of God's love personified, and recognize His spark is woven and intertwined within each of you. Be mindful of the fact that God is not, nor has He ever been, separate from you. If He were, creation would be null and void. This is why creation ebbs and flows through the avenue of free will, as it governs your thinking mind and belief systems. This is where the father energy will support you just as the mother energy does. They are a team, and they parent in tandem.

The Universe is a vast expansion of energy where all things are created. The planted seed of God the Father, in the womb of the Universal Mother, becomes the spark of creation within you. God is the gateway to this spiritual womb, and He allows you to explore this part of your consciousness free of charge. It is through the power of the Universe that your spark of creation, supported by the Father's influence, has a place to grow. Whatever it is that you fancy is yours, as God gives freely to you. Yet, it is through the power of your own actions that will create your current reality. You will get multiple chances to get it right as you are guided by God the Father, to allow creation a palpable outlet within the womb of the mother energy. He selflessly allows you the freedom to use the Universe to grow within, and in Him.

To sum it up, God gave you free will to use as you choose. Just as you were created by God within the Universe, it is God's love that sustains you and your creative endeavors. God will never close the door on you, and His love for you allows you the freedom of choice. This is where God gives you the strength to move forward in your own creations. As your soul evolves and grows within the loving arms of the Universal Mother, you will find God in the details.

The voice of wisdom whispers to us that when you teach a child to fish, they will never go hungry. Yet it is the child who is overindulged that will wither upon the vine. This is where your human moms and dads have helped to shape your future, as they taught you how to survive in a tangible world. This is also where the spiritual aspect of the mother/father energy supports you and they become a cohesive team. They guide you towards utilizing the internal place within, that houses all creation. Too many have been taught that the only way to gain the Kingdom of Heaven is to abandon self-abundance, but that is not the way God intended it to be. Think back to when you were a child – what did you want to be when you grew up? Now take a look and see how those things have come to pass.

Prosperity is a constant flow of experiences that make the person/soul unified. When a feeling of fulfillment is achieved, a tangible experience is created, and prosperity flows freely. When you are striving for success, it is paid in some form or fashion. Money is a great example of the end result of prosperity, and it is your own beliefs around money that become relevant here. Some people believe that money is the root of all evil. They are taught that to be rich in spirit you need to be poor in nature/wealth. The old saying, "I would rather be poor and happy than rich and miserable" comes to mind here. What you personally believe about money today is where your current truth is revealed. Your divine spark is asking you not to allow the true path towards being soulfully abundant (i.e., your own creative nature) to get lost in the fog. God gave to each of His children a way to reap the rewards created through the womb of the Universal Mother, and so it should be applied.

The difference between abundance and prosperity is this:

Abundance is a universal principle and available through a free flow of energy. This can be compared to what you felt and experienced as a child using your imagination. This element is never depleted and has always been available for you to access at will.

Prosperity is the tangible result of your endeavors and allows you to express yourself, and exchange that expression in the form of worth/wealth. In order to experience prosperity, you will need to act on your intentions to create through what is known as the gateway of abundance.

The playground of the Universal Mother (Abundance), supported by God's Divine Spark within you (Prosperity), is lined with gold. This is where you, the human being, become a co-creator within the Universal Mother's playground. It is where the tapestry of life is woven and sewn together.

Imagine when the young person grows into the beautiful young adult. Their life filled with the ups and downs of experiences that were activated through the gift of free will. As the adult grows, their life at times is experienced with a partner. This is where they will share their sum total of experiences thus far with one another, and where companionship becomes the gateway to their elder years. The elders' experiences become the sparkle of grey within their hair and the smile lines around their wisdom-filled eyes. They are now filled with omnipresent knowledge and their visits to the playground of the Universal Mother are purposeful. They visit as a way to share the wealth with those who have yet to experience what they have. The elder becomes the giver of wisdom and the taker of gratitude. They are abundantly prosperous, and they know much about the ins and outs to life's great mysteries, and so do you.

It all boils down to this: abundance becomes an alignment within the body, mind, and soul of each person. It is the gateway toward prosperity, and when the alignment is solid, prosperity will flow freely and in abundance. When this happens, you will recognize that you have become "Soulfully Abundant."

Patricia Horton, known to some as the "Spirit Scribe," is an author, spiritual mentor, and medium whose mission is to share her knowledge and wisdom to touch the hearts of the spiritually curious. To learn more about her work, visit:

innereyeconnections.com

LIVE YOUR PROSPEROUS LIFE

Melissa Jones

What is prosperity? Honestly, when I considered contributing to this book my first thought was, *I don't have a big enough dollar figure in the bank to talk about it.* And besides, what could I possibly say about the subject that seven thousand other people have not said already? Doubt and fear – my two least favorite things – crept in, and I had to take a hard look at them and ask, "Where is this coming from?" I needed to remind myself that prosperity is a frame of mind, a way of being.

I don't tell this story often (I don't want it to be the soundtrack of my life), but about five years ago I was in a nasty car accident. Of my fourteen days in ICU, I recall very little other than hazy moments with my mom, my sister, my son, and three specific friends. I had suffered a traumatic brain injury and as a result could not do things I had been doing and taking for granted since I was a toddler: getting out of bed, walking, and going to the bathroom unassisted. I also could not remember words or write. All this was in addition to the physical injuries, including broken ribs, a lacerated liver, and a punctured lung. I came home on a walker, graduated to a cane. Spent months in physical therapy and having brain scans. Breathing was difficult with those broken ribs, not to mention I had zero balance for any kind of yoga practice. Coming back to the breath — well, that was a chore. It hurt.

I spent a minute focusing on what I did not have. I might have had a giant pity party... can't walk, can't write, can't breathe, can't practice yoga. The wreck happened in January, I sat in suffering (optional, by the way), until fall. Then my sister was moving, and I helped her. I drove for the first time in nine months. I lifted boxes and shuffled stuff. There was a yoga festival; we went as vendors and I taught a class on essential oils. I helped with social media graphics and website things. I got a new job in Tempe that started in October, and I moved there with my son because no one really trusted me living alone. We got an apartment close to my job and I walked every day to work. I also walked the dog; my movement improved. I still could not step back for warrior pose, but motivating forward was helping.

Our financial situation was pretty tight. I changed jobs three times in Tempe, each time making a little bit more money. I took on side jobs, designed logos, built websites. I sold essential oils. I hustled. I decided to move closer to work, and the rent for a one-bedroom was nearly what we had been paying for our two-bedroom (and splitting it). I took a good hard look at the budget and decided the two to three hours per day I would not be spending on the freeway could be used to do more freelance work (plus, I would be saving on gas) so I gulped and signed. Wow... living on my own with a fat number to pay for rent every month, by myself. I believed I could do it; I took that leap of faith.

My point in sharing that story is that I am a BIG believer in affirmations. I use essential oils to set my intentions for the day. I have written on my whiteboard (where I keep track of my projects), "I AM a magnet for financial prosperity and abundance." I write it every month on my desk calendar. I doodle it. I believe that prosperity is a mindset and a vibration and I intentionally tap into that vibration. Today, I am now in a bigger apartment in the same complex (so I have dedicated office space). I write an even bigger rent check every month. Does it all boil down to using the "right" essential oils in my diffuser and repeating some positive mantras? Is that the secret sauce? Do you need to do things that scare the nonsense out of you in order to enjoy a prosperous life? Well, kind of.

I have been a student of metaphysics since the seventies... holy cow, that is a long time. When I don't trust, when I don't allow, things just don't seem to go my way. I utilize affirmations, essential oils, aromatherapy, plant medicine, yoga, and meditation to help me... daily. Here are some tools and essential oils to help get you into a prosperity mindset.

Set Goals

Yep, big fat hairy goals. Go ahead, write down that number – the big one. List the places you want to visit. Look at houses you want to buy. Write out things you want to achieve. It isn't all about the number in your bank account, but having extra money makes most things easier to do. Write those goals down, and then write them some more. As you reach one goal, choose the next one. Having goals is a cornerstone of prosperity teaching.

- Abundance – a fantastic manifesting blend – helps attract wealth and health in our lives; release emotions of "not enoughness" and worry, and let go of scarcity and poverty consciousness. This blend helps to open and balance the root (safety) and heart (love) chakras.

- Orange – helps to promote feelings of peace. It releases self-judgment, obsessions, and fears so the emotional body can be restored and balanced. Orange opens and balances the solar plexus (ego) and sacral (creativity) chakras and is great for people with perfectionist tendencies.

Take Action

Want a nicer apartment (or house or car)? The key is saying yes. Yes to the side work. Yes to the opportunities to earn a little extra money. Yes to teaching that class, or designing that logo. Yes to the promotion. This puts you in the mindset of allowing opportunities as they come. I certainly don't want to tell the Universe or God or the Divine, "No thanks, I have enough money, thank you." So keep that channel open. Set smart goals and bite-size the steps if completing the task is overwhelming.

- Grapefruit – a great oil for taking action. It is cleansing to the aura and mental body, which helps release confusion and mental chatter. Grapefruit helps us restore our own power and claim our spiritual purpose. It energizes the solar plexus chakra (ego) and expands the heart space.

The Importance of Gratitude

Being grateful for where you are today makes getting where you are going easier and much more enjoyable. Think of it this way: when you gripe and complain or are walking around with resentment, you are symbolically walking around with closed fists and a closed-off heart. Now think of walking in a gratitude space. Perhaps your hands and heart are more open, ready to receive.

- Gratitude – This blend promotes the emotions of gratefulness, thankfulness, and appreciation so we can more easily open ourselves up to receiving our gifts and blessings. I use this oil a lot and I love just a bit on my wrist so I can inhale frequently!

Affirmations

For each of your goals, write an affirmation. For example, if your goal is to have $25,000 in savings you might write, "I now have $25,000 in my savings account at XYZ bank." It might not be true at the moment you write it, but remember, we are working on your mindset here. We are envisioning your future. Write your affirmations, and write them again. I put mine on colored sticky notes and then stick them all over my apartment. I repeat them in the morning when I am setting my intentions for the day, and when I see those notes.

- Envision – Use this powerful oil to awaken and inspire your dreams and goals. It releases the fear of moving forward if you feel stuck. Looking for help with procrastination and motivation? It also gets us out of that left brain mentality and opens the randomness of the right brain, where creativity and intuition flow. Envision balances the throat chakra.

Find Success Partners

Join a mastermind group. Get a life coach. Find your tribe that can celebrate your successes and cheer you on. Think about the people you spend the most time with, do they support your goals? I attended a seminar one time where the speaker was talking about balcony people and basement people. Spend more time with balcony people. Lack is a mindset, and if you are spending time with people who have lack mentality (i.e. who say, "I couldn't possibly afford that.") it is hard to remain in an abundant mindset.

- Inner Child – This blend helps us to reconnect with our inner child or inner self that is at the core of who we are. Some of us may subconsciously still be trying to please our parents, our teachers, or boss, instead of really looking at ourselves. Calming to the mind, this oil also balances the lower three chakras: root, sacral, and solar plexus.

Determination

We all have setbacks (think about the car accident); we all have those days when the weight of the world, or hearing of a friend's loss or some other tragedy gets to us. Allow yourself time in the "ick" of it. Set a timer. Then change up the energy, put on some dance party music, change up the oils in your diffuser, or grab a bottle of lemon essential oil, and just directly inhale from the bottle. Lighten the mood, lighten your load.

- Lemon – is cleansing to the mind and spirit; it releases patterning and opens the heart center, which results in joy and hopefulness with clear thought. Lemon will help people and animals stay very present. I love to switch it up and sometimes use jade lemon.

If you have questions about the safe use of essential oils, please reach out. I have a cat, I have a dog, and I still diffuse oils every day.

Fast forward to today. My sister and I started Hippie Soul Wellness. We developed a sleeping supplement (because absolutely everyone needs better sleep) in addition to the other modalities we already practice. We are super excited about the launch of our product, Melt Into Zzz, and are working on getting that into a national grocery chain.

Make the plans, write out the big hairy goals, with the scary number. Take the leap of faith. Do it. Live your prosperous life.

Born and raised in the Sonoran Desert, **Melissa Jones** has a life-long love and appreciation for the benefits of plant medicine. Her favorite desert plant is chaparral or *Larrea tridentata*, especially after the summer monsoon storms. The smell is unforgettable. She studied at the Southwest Institute of Healing Arts and is a registered herbalist, aromatherapist, and RYT500, having completed more five hundred hours of yoga training. When she is not formulating a tea, making essential oil blends, you can find her with her camera taking photos of plants and nature, and occasionally people. As a graphic artist, website builder, and social media manager, she spends most of her daytime hours in front of the computer. In her free time, she and her sister developed and launched Hippie Soul Wellness, which provides herbal consultations, tea blends, essential oils, and life coaching. If you are in need of essential oils, Melt Into Zzz, or an amazing tea blend, visit our website:

hippiesoulwellness.com

THE GIFT OF MY BEAUTIFUL WHISPERS
Amy Kokoles

As I sit here searching for the exact right words to say, I'm stopped dead in my tracks. I hear her calling to me, begging me to speak the words that are on my heart. She is lovingly asking me to allow myself to be seen, and heard, and to shine as my most beautiful authentic self. She is my constant, my deep knowing that I am being called to more, so much more, than I ever dare allow myself to dream. She is my Beautiful Whisper.

The reason I'm here is to share my journey of becoming my most beautiful authentic self. We all have our own journey to becoming, a path that is uniquely ours. We may not know how to start, but if we get quiet and listen our soul will whisper the way. My journey started with the knowing that I needed something different. I wanted to be seen, feel loved, and know that my presence in this world was needed, and that I was enough. As I followed my path, I had no idea where I was going to end up, but I knew that I would never be the same again. And for that I am eternally grateful.

My hope is that as you read my story, you can listen to your own soul's beautiful whisper, so you can begin to trust the process and allow yourself to flow into the most amazing dance of self-love and self-worth. And, that as you finally choose to stand and shine in your authenticity, you will realize that this is the most precious gift you have ever given yourself.

My four siblings and I lived with my mom in a three-bedroom ranch house that was small and lacked any privacy. My dad left when I was five and he was mostly nonexistent in our lives, although I was close to his mother, Grandmom.

My entire life I felt as though I didn't fit in, especially in my family. I always felt different, invisible at times, not totally loved or understood. I was labeled; to be honest, all five of us were assigned a label in my family. I'm not sure how or why it started but our labels are still being used today. My label was the "family outcast," and I always hated being referred to that way. I just desperately wanted to be me – no labels, just me. I had something inside me that kept whispering, *There has to be more.* Yet every time I got the courage to try to break free and leave my label behind I was quickly put back in my place.

Growing up I had a few very close girlfriends who meant the world to me. I spent so much time at their houses that I felt like their families were mine. I felt loved and accepted by each of them and so secure knowing I could just be me. Unfortunately, once we got to high school it all fell apart. We tried to stay connected, but things had changed. The support system I had known, loved, and needed was gone.

During high school I got involved in working, dating, and other different activities to keep myself busy. I surrounded myself with my new friends, hoping they would fill the void I was feeling and, after a while, I settled in and began to enjoy life again. Yet inside, that whisper continued to tell me there was more.

I found myself craving alone time, needing to be in a quiet space where I could just be. I remember so many nights getting in my car and just driving for hours and hours with no destination in mind.

During all my driving around I remember talking to myself, to God, and to the angels and asking what my life was all about. Why was I so lonely, why were things not working out like I wanted? I begged and pleaded for answers and yet they never seemed to come. The lack of answers just made me feel even more invisible, even lonelier. After I graduated from high school, I again lost my support system. I sought out people who really weren't good for me just so I could have the connection that I so desperately needed. As I entered college, I could see the same patterns I had been avoiding coming back into my life.

Once again I was driving around, begging, pleading, and bargaining, pouring my heart out to whoever was "up there" listening, but still I got no response… or so I thought. During this whole time, in fact, almost every single time I had these "talks," I would get a whisper deep inside. This whisper was just loud enough to get me to pause, if only for a moment.

I tried to avoid my feelings with classes, working, dating, and partying. But no matter how hard I tried, the loneliness and feelings of being invisible and misunderstood and unloved were still there. As I made my way through college, I started to feel different, more comfortable in my own skin and my worth. The better I started to feel about myself, the more I started to push back against my family and their perception of me as the "outcast." Unfortunately, I never could quite break free of the label.

By the time I graduated, I felt on top of the world. Those feelings I had carried with me for all those years were finally gone. They eventually returned, however, and I went back to spending a lot of time alone. I wanted things to be different, I kept hoping, praying, begging for things to change. This time, when I heard that familiar whisper, I listened. And as I did, I allowed everything I had been feeling my entire life to wash over me like a tidal wave. I realized it was time for me to do something different.

I began reading books, journaling, and talking to God, my angels and any other beings that were out there. I started unpacking all the lies that I told myself, all the lies I had let myself believe. I realized that I really was the "family outcast," but now instead of fighting it, I totally embraced it!

I met and married the love of my life, John. He loves and supports me and allows me to be myself, always. Having his love and support has allowed me to trust myself enough to go deeper on my path to find my authentic self.

I had remained close to Grandmom; we talked several times a week and John and I visited her often. When she passed away, though I was sad, I was incredibly grateful that I had been able to have such a wonderful relationship with her. After her funeral, my dad asked if I would help clean out Grandmom's house. I agreed and started spending time with a man who, though biologically related to me, was a stranger.

As my dad and I grew close, I could see so much of myself in him. At the same time, my relationship with my mom and siblings quickly started to fall apart. I realized that even though I loved them, they were – and still are – incapable of being a loving, supportive force in my life. My mom was my best friend and I suspect she felt I had betrayed her by having a relationship with the man who had left us all those years ago. I tried to hold on to whatever was left between us, but it was in vain. Finally, in sheer devastation, I dropped to my knees and let them all go.

As I sat with all of this and tried to process my new normal, I could feel myself starting to change. I began to enjoy the freedom that I felt from being able to be me. I had finally escaped the label, which was designed to control me and keep me small. For the first time in my life, I was stepping out and shining as me, the beautifully flawed outcast who never fit in.

I continued my relationship with my dad, and I absolutely cherished it. He saw me not as a label but as a completely whole person. It's funny how many times I knew exactly what he was thinking without a single word. Then came the day I had to tell him he was dying. My dad, who was so strong physically and spiritually, cried in desperation when I broke the news. He became so angry with me that he denied my words and told me to get out of his hospital room.

We struggled for a few weeks with our relationship before finally getting back on solid ground. I was with my dad until the end, and I am so happy that I trusted myself enough to be vulnerable with him.

By allowing my dad into my life I got to experience unconditional love from a parent.

I am so grateful that I got to know and love my dad. Our relationship healed me in ways I never knew I was broken.

As I closed out my dad's life and began looking at myself with a deeper love and understanding, I realized that those whispers, my whispers, had been there all along. For every prayer I said, every question I asked, I always got an answer. I just didn't know it at the time.

After so many years of trying and failing, more times than I'll probably ever admit, I finally found what was missing. *It was my beautiful, authentic self.* I realized that I was enough; in fact, I was more than enough, and that I have value just because I am me. I'm so happy that I finally listened to the whispers deep inside. The whispers that called me to stand in my authenticity, and to shine my beautiful light to the world. For all that I was, and all that I have become, I am so eternally grateful to my Beautiful Whispers.

Amy Kokoles is a writer, philanthropist, and certified angel guide. From an early age Amy was called to follow her heart and do things her way. She loves to challenge herself, which led her to say yes when the opportunity to contribute to this book appeared. She has spent the last several years volunteering in her community, for which she received The President's Volunteer Service Award and has been interviewed for several articles and an international podcast.

As part of her spiritual journey and service to others, Amy created the Facebook group, **Becoming You ~ Beautiful Whispers**, a sacred space for women that allows them to stand in their authenticity while being supported and loved as their most beautiful selves.

Amy has a deep love of nature, especially thunderstorms and the ocean, as they call to her heart and soul. She is married to her best friend and partner in crime, John. They live in the suburbs of Philadelphia, Pennsylvania with their much-loved fur babies.

amykokoles@gmail.com

LET GO AND PROSPER

Ghene't Lee-Yong

For most of my adult life I have struggled with finances. Try as I might to save so I could budget and plan, I always came up short. I would see other people around me prosper. They would go from living in an apartment to buying their first home to selling and buying a second. These were people that at first I thought were rich. However, as I got to know them better, I realized they were not in a very different income range; in fact, some of them made less annually than my husband and I did. What was this magic? Why couldn't we make the same moves? I felt alone in this struggle and could not understand how other people were "doing it" and we were not.

I listened when I was told, "Well, they must be getting money from their parents. Or, "They probably put it all on credit cards. We don't use credit cards." Or, "They're probably getting money under the table." This, I guess, somehow implied that our state of constant struggle was noble because we were not "stooping" to these levels to get ahead. I listened when I was told that material wealth did not mean spiritual wealth and that we were connected spiritually and spirituality mattered more than anything else.

I listened to these scripts for a very long time until I began writing down instances when we were short on money. Times when I put money aside and then it was spent without my consent. Times when we could not pay the rent or electricity or water bills. The number of times we had to move from place to place. I started calculating the cost of the moves, the money that was spent without my input. I also calculated our annual income and made a budget based on that. What I found was shocking. On paper we should not only be able to afford the necessities, we should have had extra left over for savings.

Now I was faced with letting go of the false reality I was living in. Letting go of denial. In fact, I had to let go of many things – mainly, my idea that being a divorced mom of two was somehow shameful. That I could not do it on my own. That it was my duty to be a good wife and stay married no matter what. That being prosperous meant making a certain amount, an amount I could never achieve. The act of releasing was not easy and it took years to get to the action that led to my abundance.

I had to be honest with myself about the truth of our situation. What was really happening? Where was the money going? And… how was this issue with money a reflection of other issues in the marriage and family dynamic? The idea that spirituality and financial prosperity are two separate things is false. All are tied in the same knot. Sometimes the only way for our Higher Power to tell us something is very wrong in our lives is to allow financial turmoil to surface so we can begin to face the problem. We live in a physical plane with money as our energy currency. Nothing makes us stop and take pause faster than an interruption in the flow of that physical energy.

Being honest and owning my part in the financial disparity I lived in meant facing the reality of my spouse's substance abuse, how it affected his behavior towards me and the children, and my part in enabling that. I had to look at how that affected us not only financially, but spiritually, physically, mentally, and socially. Once I was able to accept this, I was then in a position to make some tough choices. It was not easy and it was not overnight. Eventually, for the sanity and well-being of all involved, I had to separate. That was the summer of 2019.

In a matter of three years, I have gone from living in an apartment to owning a home on three acres of land. I went from working a job that paid less than thirty-five thousand a year and took all of my time to working from home making more than seventy thousand a year. *In three years, I doubled my income and more than doubled my living space!* On top of that I increased the sense of peace and tranquility in my family life. I am building strong relationships with my children and have reconnected with my family of origin. Looking back, I can see the dramatic effect of prayerful, tearful choices. At that moment, what I saw was a rock wall that I had to climb with two children in tow and tons of baggage weighing me down.

I often think of the act of leaving was what led me to where I am now, but the truth is it started way before that. Years before 2019 I started to move through a process, one I was unaware of, to get to this point. This was a process of Letting Go. Letting go took time and it took four important steps: **Honesty, Defining, Receiving,** and **Action.**

1. I had to be **Honest** about what the real root of my financial instability was and accept this as fact, despite what anyone else said.

2. I had to **Define** what I truly believed prosperity was. I had to align with what my Higher Power and higher self saw as prosperity. I had to get clear about what would truly bring joy to my life and the lives of my children.

3. I had to **Receive.** This meant believing I could make the right choices and follow through. Being open to new

ways of doing things. Being willing to trust my Higher Power. Learning to say no to things that did not serve me. Learning to say yes to things that could benefit me.

4. I had to **Act**. There were several actions that needed to be taken. I left a hurtful relationship. I left a job that did not provide what I needed. I interviewed for higher-paying jobs. I moved from the city to a rural area. I made quality time with my children and my family of origin.

I found in my search that prosperity does not elude us because we do not make enough money, or the system is set against us, or that we are unworthy of living a good life. I found that prosperity eludes us because our definition of prosperity is in misalignment with what prosperity truly is. Our higher selves and our Higher Power have a true definition of what prosperity is for us and our conscious mind and outside influences have another view. When we continue to strive and struggle for a life of success that does not align with our inner truth, we can never achieve the level of prosperity we desire.

We lack prosperity because we give our power away to false scripts and beliefs handed down to us by our parents, friends, teachers, spouses, media, and governments. We live in lack because we do not believe we can ever achieve what we want, so why bother trying. This is a subconscious thought, one we are often unaware of, and it sabotages right choices and decisions. It holds us to routines, places, and people that do not serve our higher good and prevent us from moving toward financial stability.

Letting go is an ongoing process that is undertaken in progression. Give it time and consistency and you will see change. You will look back and say, "How did that happen?" It happens with honesty, defining, receiving and action.

Prosperity Activity

Journal

It will be important to keep a journal. This can be a note app or a file in your laptop. This journal is for you. Your eyes only. It is a way of putting your truth on paper, organizing your thoughts, and clearing your mind.

Write about what your situation is now. Exactly as it is. No judgment, this is just a state of what is. Express how this makes you feel. Be honest. Is it frustration? Are you mostly happy but feel there is another level? Are you angry? There is no wrong emotion. There is no wrong feeling.

Write in your journal what you define as prosperity, wealth, success. Again, there is no judgment. This is *your* definition. Is it an amount? Is it a certain type of home or location? There could be many contradicting things. That is okay as well. As time goes on you will begin to narrow down what you truly want.

Nature Immersion

After you journal, you will need to move the energies that just flowed through you. Go for a walk, swim, hike, jog, et cetera. You do not necessarily need to think about what you journal, just keep it in the back of your mind. Observe nature around you and notice its abundance. Even in highly urban areas, notice that nature finds a way to present itself. Notice that when it does it does so in fantastic and opulent ways. Take pictures or just try to remember what you see.

Journal

Think about how you can show up in small but opulent ways. Write about what you saw as a way to enter into a free-writing state. Begin writing whatever comes to mind for as long as you are led to or set a timer for the amount of time you are able. Write one thing you can and are willing to immediately change. Basically, what is the next positive step up?

Meditate

Take time several times during the week to meditate. Listen for guidance on what action you should take. Ask to be open to seeing opportunities that maybe you would not have seen before. A simple mediation example is

God,

Open my eyes so I can see new and abundant opportunities

Open my heart so I can receive and be available

Guide my steps to allow me to be in the right places
at the right times

Give me courage to right action

All for my highest good and the highest good
for all involved.

Repeat this activity weekly if you can. You will notice how your ideas of prosperity change and you will also start to prioritize what is most important, for now, to get you to the next level of success. There is no race. Just go one day at a time, one step at a time.

Let Go and Prosper.

Ghene't Lee-Yong, mother of two, is the author of the workbook *Nature Immersion Six Weeks to a Healthier Mind, Body, and Spirit.* She earned her Bachelors of Cognitive Science and has certificates in Nature Therapy, Wilderness First Aide and Rescue and Nutrition Health Coaching. Ghene't is the owner of Strongereveryday1111 and a small start-up farm in Tennessee. She leads therapeutic hikes and nature immersive experiences for groups and individuals called Healing Hikes. She is dedicated to helping people find self-love and balance in their daily lives through nature immersion, meditation and intentional movement and eating. Ghene't believes that all success in all areas of life start with self-love and acceptance. Remote and In-person, she has helped many people achieve weight loss and personal goals that lead to a higher sense of personal fulfilment.

strongereveryday111.com

THE AUDACITY TO BELIEVE
Amber Marie

For as long as I can remember I have held myself back from following my heart based on others' opinions and beliefs. I have quit many things in my life because of others thoughts and opinions, and I gave up and shifted my whole world around to fit into the box of their ideas about my life and journey. All of these people loved me, so of course they wanted what they thought was best for me – who doesn't want to see their child, friend, loved one thrive and want to do their best to help them avoid painful pitfalls? I have also done this to others in my life as well. It wasn't until a life-changing experience that I realized how codependent I had become on everyone around me, and how much I had ignored my own inner guidance because it did not align with them.

Something needed to change, and though I knew I couldn't change anyone else, I could change myself by doing the inner work I had been avoiding. Hell, I had spent so much of my life avoiding pain and emotion and now there I was, welcoming it to the surface so I could shine light on it. What the fuck was I thinking?! Was I losing my mind? Some may think so, and maybe I was, but it was the best thing I ever did for myself and I want others to do the same so they can experience the freedom of releasing that which is hidden within the shadows.

I have learned so much about myself in the last six months of doing this deep inner work that I welcome the emotions today with more ease and flow than ever before. Everything within us wants to be seen, heard, felt, and honored, including the deepest, darkest secrets we have kept hidden within ourselves out of fear of being shamed or condemned by those we love.

Investing in Yourself

Many of you may have been to Sedona, or have heard of it and all its magic. I have been to Sedona three times in my life, twice within the last six months. After that life-changing experience that was the catalyst for my deep dive into myself, I went to a retreat held by a woman I absolutely love and adore, Sunny Dawn Johnston. Have you heard of her? If not, check her out! As someone who lived in fear for so long, investing in myself was not at the top of my priority list. However, this time was different! I secured my deposit for the retreat, hands shaking, tears flooding my face, and my mind going absolutely insane! Here are some of the things my mind was telling me:

"What the fuck are you doing?"

"Who do you think you are? You aren't supposed to spend money like this on yourself."

"You don't have that kind of money!"

"What will they think?"

"Girl, you are worried about rent and you're doing this… 51/50, your ass!"

And these are just a few, for as you've probably realized our minds spit out thousands of thoughts and some in a matter of seconds. These were the thoughts that stuck out to me. These were the ones I had always showed up for me any time I even had the inspiration to do something for myself. Can you relate to the racing thoughts any time you followed your heart and stepped out of the comfort zone and into the growth zone? I am sure you know exactly what I am sharing with you.

After making this deposit I decided to share with a few women in my sacred circle, where I feel safe and free to be one hundred percent me. They all celebrated me taking this leap of investing in myself. Talk about feeling supported! Support shows up in a variety of ways, and the amount of support I received from these Soul SiSTARS was profound. I was reminded that prosperity shows up in so many ways other than just the digits in our bank accounts. I had taken a leap and the Universe showed up, celebrating and supporting me for trusting the guidance and mustering up the courage despite what my negative self-talk was telling me. I had the audacity to BELIEVE in the unknown and, let me tell you, it was one of the best investments I have ever made!

The Sedona Experience

When I arrived in Arizona, I was blessed with the opportunity to meet some of my Soul SiSTARS *in real life!* In the world of COVID we had discovered that no matter where we are in the world, we always have ways to connect. Most of the women at the retreat I first met online, and though that was an incredible experience I felt so blessed to receive the gift of an in-person connection.

Before going to Sedona, I made a promise to myself that no matter what came up I was going to walk through it. I wasn't going to hold back; I wasn't going to shrink and keep myself small; I was going to speak even when my throat was trying to keep my quiet. And I did just that; I still had a fear of speaking up and Spirit definitely helped me walk through it. I am going to share my experiences and the biggest lesson I learned while in this sacred container with a group of powerful, wise, magical women from all different walks of life.

My HUGE a-ha moment on the retreat was after an exercise that was extremely uncomfortable and profound at the same time. We had partners and we sat across from each other without saying a word, staring into each other's eyes while touching our partner's face. There were tons of tears and loads of awareness. When you sit with someone and look into their eyes you see their true essence on a deeper level. You see their soul, feel their soul, hear their soul, and honor the journey they have been through.

Then came part two of this experience, when we were blindfolded and asked to find our partner based on the connection we developed during our soul-gazing exercise. There was a group of us navigating through the darkness relying only on this energetic connection. During this time I felt I connected with my partner a few times, but the outside noise took me off my path; I let my outside senses override my intuition, and my partner and I were the last in the group to connect. Afterward, we were asked to journal in order to share our takeaways with the group. This is where I realized the connection between this experience and the vast majority of my life: I had *always* allowed the outside noise to overpower my owner inner guidance system, my intuition. Tears rolled down my face as I reflected on the many times in my life when I felt guided to do something and didn't follow through. Can you relate to feeling called to do something or share something but allowed the doubt and outside opinions stop you? I realized on a deeper level the importance of trusting the guidance we receive from Spirit. It is our journey, isn't it? There is nothing wrong with seeking counsel, however, when we only rely on the counsel of others we tend to take more detours, at least this has been my experience.

I made a choice during the retreat to not discredit my own intuition based on another's guidance. Not one more time would I ignore that voice within guiding me, the messages my body gives me, or the synchronicity that Spirit shows me on a consistent basis. I chose to have the audacity to believe in my intuition, no matter what!

If you have ever heard of Sunny's retreats being life-changing, they TRULY are, my friends! We spent four days connecting, going within, being vulnerable, laughing, dancing, hiking, singing (some really well, some not so...), and embracing one another in the sacredness of sisterhood! I was the youngest woman there and I received the beautiful gift of having ten more mothers in my life and the most badass grandma anyone could ask for (if they are reading this, they know who they are!). I am eternally grateful for each and every one of those women for the space they held for me and for one another, and so much more than any words can describe.

I ask you the follow questions, SiSTAR:

1. What are you willing to no longer do?

2. What are you willing to do to show up for yourself?

3. What is one thing you can commit to yourself in order to make your dreams come true?

4. How are you willing to honor yourself and the guidance you receive from Spirit?

These are questions I ask myself nearly every day since the catalyst that helped change my life and perspective. I want you to know that this is a journey and it's a practice, so on those days that feel dark and heavy, give yourself grace. Lean into the lessons being presented to you; and just like you show up for others, show up for yourself! Your beautiful soul deserves to have the Audacity to Believe in the prosperous opportunities that are continuously showing up in your life every moment of every day!

There are so many women in the world who have sacrificed the truth of who we are and do what we are told to avoid making waves. Waves are beautiful, powerful, and transformative. Look at the ocean – She is vast, glorious, free, and limitless, and She lets nothing stop her from reaching the shoreline! You wild women are also all of this and so much more! We are here for a reason and part of that is to stop playing small and believe in the abundance of life that is all around you. I challenge you, SiSTAR, to believe in yourself, trust your intuition, open your heart to receive, and allow the miracles to unfold in your life because they will!

Amber Marie is a Reiki healer, certified life coach, virtual assistant, and intuitive guide helping others create their own magic in this world. She studied at Southwest Institute of Healing Arts, however, the best education she has received is through life experiences. A self-described "compassionate rebel," Amber Marie is dedicated to holding space for other women as they discover and honor their true essence. After spending years hiding from the world, she is stepping out to share her gifts, helping bring more connection, authenticity, and healing.

Amber Marie relocated from North Dakota to Sacramento, California, where she lives with her beautiful daughter, her fur baby, and the love of her life.

amber@alignedassistance.com

FINDING THE GIFTS IN GRIEF & LOSS

Paula Meyer

It seems like a contradiction to say that grief and loss provide gifts, yet when I look back on the losses I have experienced in the last several years – really throughout my life – I have found so many. So many hidden gems and pearls that revealed who I really am. And I'm no different from you. We all have experienced losses throughout our lives that have created the people we are today, in this very moment. These losses are valuable contributions to the forming of us as humans and as spiritual beings. I want to take you through some of these losses and the gifts I've discovered as a result. Sometimes it took many years and many tears to discover the gift, yet even in that long walk of denial there were elements that served me in the long run.

Indeed, most of the time when the wound of a loss is fresh and raw, it's hard to see any gifts. When I find myself in that painful spot, I pause and ask myself, "If I were to pretend to find the gift in it, what might that look like?" And then I write down two or three possibilities. When I was able to look at them from the perspective of child-like curiosity and wonderment, the whole landscape shifted in a way that allowed me to reframe my experience.

Here are further questions I've asked that allowed me to be more introspective and open my mind to alternative perspectives. I have found that to answer these questions requires us to be vulnerable, which makes space to rewrite the story we have been telling ourselves.

- What meaning did I assign to this painful experience? Are there other meanings that I could have assigned to it? You must be willing to see other ways of looking at it. If you find this difficult, you might try to find a quiet space, tune into your Spirit, and ask, "What other ways could I see this situation that does not label me in a negative way?"

- What did it show me about ME? What was my reaction and did it come from fear or love?

- What did it show me about the other people in the experience? Did my experience match those of the others? Many times, our shared experiences are very different.

- What feelings did I feel at the time? Were they really true?

Now, on to a couple of examples from my own life – one from childhood and one much more recent – so you can see the answers to some of the questions above.

Childhood-Defining Experience: Donny Osmond Album

Back in the early '70s, when Donny Osmond was all the rage, I desperately wanted his album. It was nearing Christmas and back then we used to do a gift exchange with our extended family. My aunt drew my name and my mom asked me for ideas. I only had one request – the album – and I was so excited in anticipation of receiving it! I couldn't wait to play the record! When the evening of the gift exchange arrived, we began to take turns opening our gifts.

When it was my turn, I received a small, beautifully wrapped box from my aunt. I was crushed! It obviously wasn't the album I had asked for. I quietly opened it to find a beautiful watch. I thanked my aunt, then quickly disappeared to my room and burst into tears. My mom followed me, and when I told her what was wrong she got angry with me. In my little-girl mind, I decided in that moment that what I had to say was not important, that I never got what I asked for, and thus I didn't matter. I carried that with me my whole life. Certainly, there were many other experiences that helped to create this belief, not just this one Donny Osmond moment. But this one carried a whole lot of weight, even though I had forgotten about it in my later years.

While attending a workshop in 2008, we were asked to think about a childhood experience that created limiting beliefs in our adulthood. I remembered the Donny Osmond album and was surprised at how easily the anger came rushing back. We were then told to step to the left of the experience and view it from a different perspective. A possibility was that my mom forgot to tell my aunt what I wanted. The instructor asked if that experience would have carried the same meaning. Hmm, that's an interesting idea. Then we were asked to step to the right and do the same thing. The second possibility was that my mom did tell my aunt, and she decided that a watch would be more meaningful in the long run. Hmm, another very interesting idea. There were two other possibilities that I could have experienced and neither one labeled me as unworthy to be heard! That was a huge eye-opener for me.

Adulthood-Defining Experience: My husband Gary's Death

On June 1, 2018, my husband Gary died at the age of sixty-two after a four-year battle with throat cancer. It was very hard to find the gifts in his agonizing and debilitating death. It was so unfair that he died so young. I felt cheated that we didn't get to retire together.

We should have been able to grow old together. We would never share the experience of being grandparents together. How could anything good ever come out of this?

Gary and I had spent more than twenty years in spiritual self-development, so despite the pain I had a good foundation to start the process of seeing the gifts. First, I had to allow myself to feel the feelings. That was hard to do. It still is, but it has gotten easier over time. I started by looking at things that I had to learn to do myself now that Gary was gone. Things like clearing my long hair out of the shower drain (gross!), driving long distances by myself, taking personal vacations by myself, and learning to feel confident taking my car to the auto shop. There were so many things Gary took care of that I now had to learn to do myself. So I started there. I allowed myself to feel proud of those minor accomplishments. I thanked Gary for taking care of them all those years. I thanked myself for the courage to attempt them. I laughed if I didn't quite live up to Gary's standard because I knew he would be proud of me. In this way, I became proud of myself.

When I look back now, I see all the amazing people and experiences that have shown up in my life after Gary's death. So many things I have learned about myself, that I never would have learned while he was alive. There is an avalanche of gifts that I have received since he died, because I stepped into my courage and took baby steps into the unknown. I had promised him that I would live a happy life after he was gone, and now I realize that in making that promise to him, I was really making that promise to myself. And I am keeping that promise every day, knowing I deserve to be happy and free, even if I don't have a husband to share it with!

If you are struggling with any loss, big or small, I invite you to ask yourselves these questions. Be willing to look at your loss with a new set of eyes. Take off the glasses of the past, bathe your eyes in drops of love, and look at it from a curious and playful perspective. Release your inner child from those bonds that hold you both back.

From this vantage point, I see a cornucopia overflowing with all the gifts presented to me by the losses in my life. That iconic image that we use for our Thanksgiving Day celebrations is a perfect image to represent these gifts. And to re-present ourselves to them when we are experiencing a new loss. These gifts are always available to us as reminders that we can cope, we can move forward, and we can still live a wonderful and rewarding life. There will always be losses in our lives. Everyone dies, our lives change, we lose people, we leave jobs, we live through a global pandemic – the list goes on and on. There are always challenges and that's what life is all about.

Life is made up of myriad everyday experiences of all different shades and flavors. Be grateful for it all! Yes, all of it! Every single stinking, painful, horrible, beautiful, magnificent experience is what bathes us, hones us, and creates the beautiful beings we are. Just like the rivers of time have created so many majestic mountains, canyons, and caverns, all of our life experiences combine together to express who we are. It's up to us to use them ALL to create the greatest version of ourselves.

All those gifts are the prosperity the Universe has showered on us to create the ultimate gift: YOU and ME!

After becoming a widow at fifty-four, **Paula Meyer** left her job and began a year of travel to heal her heart. As her travel ended, the Covid-19 pandemic began, throwing her into the unknown just as she founded a new business. The strategies for navigating the grief of her husband's death from throat cancer also helped with the grief from the pandemic and social unrest.

Paula has thirty-plus years of experience as an event planner and contracting specialist, with twelve years in author/speaker management. She has organized and managed one hundred and fifty-one workshops around the world, and is a Certified Grief Educator through David Kessler's program.

Paula has traveled to twenty countries and forty-two US states, and her goal is to visit thirty countries and all fifty-six states and territories by the end of 2025. Her new book, *Great Loss, Greater Love: The Art & Heart of Navigating Grief*, chronicles her year of travel, and is a #1 International Bestseller on Amazon. Learn more at:

paulameyer.com

SOUL FREEDOM
Sherri "Shaw" Morgan

We, my friends, are about to embark on a little journey together. We are going to talk about fear, freedom, stress, mindset, better choices, and longevity, all for a better quality of life well into the wisdom years.

Ready? Okay, here we go!

You can't live in fear and have freedom at the same time. I mean, think about it. If you live in fear, the last thing you are is free. If you are truly free, if your mind is truly free, then the mind must be free from being in fear, right?

I am not saying that fear can never come up – of course it will. I'm saying if you are living in that fear, letting it control where you go, who you see, and what you do, then you are not free.

As a child, I was not free, at all. Fear tactics were embedded deep. I lived imprisoned by the fear of my dad. Whatever he said was law and the punishment of not doing it his way was more than I was willing to endure. His belt and my behind had our moments together and I avoided them as much as I could. He was what I feared most. Funny thing, he was also my biggest hero. I wanted to be just like him – well, the image of who I thought he was, anyway: smart, strong, tough, cool, in control.

Then, when I was fourteen, something flipped. My dad was caught in an affair and kicked out of the house. Not only did I lose my respect for him, I lost my fear of him too. We both recognized it in that one defining moment when he told me he would kill me if I came out of my brother's bedroom and I stepped into the hallway anyway. Though he didn't say another word, he realized he had lost his grip of control over me. I think he was in a tangled mix of anger and admiration. He became keenly aware that he'd raised one badass and fearless daughter.

Now that I lost my fear for the thing in life I feared most, I had very little fear of anything. I was free, my mind was free, and it felt amazing!

It's hard to define freedom because what I think it is may be different from what you think. What I do know is that freedom is my number one core value and I have sacrificed things that others think are important in order to keep it – things like not moving up at a job, not staying in a relationship, even not obtaining "stuff" to weigh me down. Infringing upon my freedom was a sure way to lose me.

You see, freedom makes my soul happy and I'm all about keeping this beautiful soul happy, healthy, and feeling alive!

Maybe it stems from my childhood experiences, but I didn't set out consciously to build my life around freedom. Somewhere along the line it just happened. When I felt into a new career or promotion, a friendship or partnership, or anything else, if it made me feel constricted, I set off in the other direction.

Our bodies tell us, you know. If we are moving in a direction that is not true to our essence, our soul will have us feeling uneasy, tight, off, drained, whatever. That's how you know you are doing something not in alignment with your spirit.

Some of us keep moving in that uneasy direction anyway. Maybe we think we should, or it's expected of us, or it'll bring us money, fame, a lover. Then we end up chasing the next thing because the last thing didn't bring us the happiness we expected. All along our soul is screaming at us that those things are not at all what we want. A free mind makes more aligned choices.

We become truly living out of alignment with our essence, and that's the opposite of freedom. We start to feel anxious, overwhelmed, exhausted, restless, and – worst of all – we forget what lights us up. We forget what feeds our beautiful souls. Pieces of our souls begin to break off.

The stress-related health issues come next – such as heart attack, breathing problems, reproductive problems, and many more.

Did you know being over-stressed can literally kill brain cells? It can shrink the part of our brain responsible for memory and learning. It messes with the synapse regulation, which will have us avoiding social interactions too.

Sharp thinking becomes a thing of the past. This damage makes it harder to think clearly and make those important life decisions. The ability to get in the right mindset becomes much more difficult, bringing you even further from what your spirit craves. More pieces of the soul depart.

All this affects our longevity. Almost all of us crave a long life, right? And not just a long life, but a life that we love right up to that final day. Active, cognitive, healthy, happy.

I wouldn't want a long life unless those final years are all quality years. I have seen far too many people spend way too many hours a day just sitting in a chair, for years, waiting to die. Well, I am not going out like that!

It doesn't have to be like that for any of us. We get to decide. The choices we make lead us to that life or they lead us to an active, adventurous, fulfilling one. Your choices today can and will determine what your capabilities will be in the future. You decide. I want you to understand, it is never too late to make better choices towards that. No matter what your past is, choosing better today will make a difference!

I had a friend whose left leg was crushed in a work accident. It happened years before I met him. Total reconstruction, metal rods for bones, fake kneecap, all of it. He was very inactive because he experienced extreme pain. I got him walking – only a few blocks at first, then longer and longer. He was amazed that the more he walked the less pain he felt. He was strengthening those muscles, and they in turn supported his knee better. Now he is an avid hiker and goes long distances, sometimes doing multiple hikes in a day. He decided to do something different, and it changed his life.

We are not destined for pain and suffering just because we age. The choices we make determine that too. I know so many people my age, and much younger, who have pain and conditions they attribute to getting older. I am fifty-six and I do not have any aches, pains, or "conditions." I'm active, adventurous, and will not stop. I choose to do the things that will continue to allow me to be dynamic and audacious right up to the day I cease to exist in this body. *I choose.* I'm not just talking about physically, but also mentally. I never stop learning; this keeps the mind young too.

What is more prosperous than feeling healthy, happy, alive, and free until the very day your gorgeous soul departs your current body?

Where to begin? Do what makes your soul happy, making choices that are in alignment with what it craves. That is what keeps the energy body balanced and healthy. The health of the energy body is everything.

Through my shamanic training, and as a shaman, I believe that all ailments come to us through an imbalance of energy. We have soul pieces we have lost, power we have given away, energies we have picked up. All keeping us out of balance.

One of the things I do to stay physically and mentally young is to make sure to keep that balance. Sometimes that means I need to pull energies back and sometimes I need to release energies that I am holding onto that don't belong to me. A shamanic healing is one way to get this done. Many of my clients have had life-changing experiences after their healings.

If you are not ready for a healing, the absolute best place to start is a daily morning walk. Make it in nature if you can, but if it must be on a treadmill in your basement, then so be it. That walk will get the blood flowing, which will get nutrients to the muscles, tissues, and brain, keeping them functioning the way they were intended to. But it's so much more than that. What it does for the mind is just as nourishing.

I like to approach the walk in one of two ways. Sometimes I do a meditative walk, listening to super-chill music, just being present. I notice all the things around me – be they things in the neighborhood I hadn't noticed before, animals on a nature walk, or, if I'm on the treadmill, the colors, shapes, objects, temperature, smells, et cetera in the room. No thinking about the day ahead or the day behind, only the here and now. When the mind wanders, I just pull it back.

The second type is to "mind dump" while walking. That could be you envisioning your day, what you want to accomplish, steps you'll take towards goals, et cetera. You can also work out in your head something that happened and you have not processed yet. That could be a negative situation, unreleased emotions, those sorts of things. Just getting it all up and out so clarity can set in and you can start your day with a free mind.

You could also combine the two. Pick a mid-point for your walk. Start with the mind dump, then at the halfway point say out loud, "I release (insert whatever came up)." During the second half of the walk get into that relaxed meditative state, ready to tackle the day with lucidity and brilliance!

I'm going to challenge you to do these walks for thirty days. I bet you see a big change in your life. Your walks may get longer, or even turn into a run. But one thing is for sure, soul freedom can be found on those walks. That's what I crave for you, that's what your spirit craves for you. Soul freedom!

You will be in control of your future. You will live more of your life from a place of freedom and clarity and less from fear and stress. Living the life aligned with your essence, with what you came here to do. You will feel alive, totally alive.

You deserve that. More than you know, you deserve that!

Sherri "Shaw" Morgan grew up in the inner city of North Minneapolis. Her life experiences demanded the deep dive into the healing path she has trekked over the last decade. No longer living small for others, she now chooses to go all in!

She has an unwavering need to build her life around freedom and adventure. This is exactly what her soul craves. It's not what she does, it's who she is.

In the Human Design world, Sherri is a manifesting generator, meaning she has several interests. The proof is in her many certifications: skincare formulator, health coach, personal trainer, photographer, shaman, psychic, and many more. She even spent a short time as a bounty hunter!

She has now settled in nicely as a longevity coach and skin care alchemist. As Sherri says of these two seemingly different paths, "Who doesn't feel alive while indulging in a luxurious face mask or looking and feeling their best by using natural skin care products that makes them glow?" And that is what her indie skincare brand, ShawBella, provides.

sherrimorgan.com

PATHWAY TO ABUNDANCE
Pat Mork

We met one summer night at a biker party. It was a case of mistaken identities. We laughed and after much beer was consumed we jumped, naked, into the lake. It was spontaneous and sexy. I went home with him that night. He called the next day and the next. By fall I had moved in. I was twenty-one. He was thirty-one.

Jeff was smart. He could fix anything. He loved to read. He had a skilled trade and owned his own townhouse. I thought I had won the lottery. One evening, we were having one of our long talks and he turned to me and said, "You are the smartest woman I know. It would be a real waste to you and the world if you didn't go back to school and finish your degree." I was floored. He saw something in me that I didn't see in myself. What a gift.

I started attending night school, taking one or two classes each semester while working full-time. At thirty-something the degree was mine. My career was going well. I was receiving another promotion.

Jeff believed in buying the best quality you can afford. Over the years, "best quality" manifested in many ways. We completely remodeled our home one room at a time. Nothing happened until the ideas were worked out and money was saved for the project. This was also where I learned that I was in fact creative. Jeff had to point out to me that there were as many of my ideas as his present throughout our home.

Though our home was lovely, our homelife had become pretty challenging. Jeff's alcoholism was taking a toll. I went to bed early every night. I woke at 5:15, was out the door by 5:30, and at the gym by 6:00. A workout and shower later, I was at the office by 8:00. By contrast, Jeff stayed up at night drinking. He came to bed after I was asleep. There were nights when I lay in bed counting double snaps as each new beer was opened. Our Saturdays started at noon, as that was the earliest he could get himself out of bed. He was also a two-plus-pack-a-day Camel Lights man. Smoking was a constant battle between us.

"How do I improve my marriage? Teach me some coping skills." By my third therapy session the inevitable question would come: "What will you do if things don't change?" That was my signal to end therapy. I was unhappy, but couldn't see myself leaving. It was too scary to contemplate. I was staying in the marriage. It was Jeff who needed changing.

I spent most of my energy managing the emotions in the house. Walking on eggshells, not doing anything that would cause an argument. Jeff was becoming more and more reclusive. Our friends were not extending invitations anymore. Jeff would get upset if I wanted to go out of town to visit family. I was more and more miserable and didn't know what to do.

I often went to psychics seeking relief and answers. One afternoon, I saw Sharon Gammell. The reading was coming to a close when she said, "There's another message from Spirit. Start taking a few dollars from every paycheck and spending them on you and you alone." She continued, "This money is for you and what makes you happy. You are not to spend it on anyone else, not even for a gift. It's not for bills. This money is to invest in you. If you don't know what to spend it on, save it. Watch and listen. Spirit will show you the way"

The next pay period, I stuffed twenty-five dollars in an envelope and hid it in my closet. I repeated this every time I got paid. Occasionally, I would spend some of it on my annual weekend away with friends. Over the years, as my income increased, the amount I put in the envelope also increased.

Then, Spirit showed me something to invest in. I heard about the Light Body meditation classes. It seemed so expensive at the time. Fortunately, I had the money stashed in my closet. Having the money avoided arguments. It also avoided my feeling guilty about spending the money. This was an investment in me.

The class changed my life. The meditations brought peace. They cleared my energy and helped release resistance and old stories. Sometimes it was painful, learning I was the one that needed to change if I wanted my life to change. Learning I was the one who needed to forgive in order for my life to improve. Learning to let go of what I don't want and focus on what I do want. As the old stories, trauma, and resistance left me, my vibration began to rise.

As my vibration was shifting and sustaining higher levels, my tolerance for negativity was dropping. There were people, places, and media that I could no longer tolerate. This was causing issues at home. It was impossible for me to handle Jeff's negativity, smoking, and drinking.

Our arguments increased. One evening after a long day at work I was greeted with a hissed, "I hate seeing your headlights come up the driveway. It reminds me how much I hated seeing my dad's headlights coming up the driveway."

How do you respond to that?

In spite of our arguments, we tried a week in Spain for our twenty-fifth anniversary. We'd never had a honeymoon and I really wanted to go to Europe so I wasn't taking no for an answer. Jeff made it clear this was my idea and it was all about me. I wasn't sure he would get on the plane. It was one of the most miserable experiences of our marriage. The details need their own chapter.

What was clear following that trip was what my future with Jeff looked like: bleak and lacking in joy.

I was forty-nine, and we were at a point in our lives where we had a little more disposable income. My dream was to continue exploring the world and having fun new adventures. Jeff had no interest.

After we returned from Spain, I joined a new meditation group. My free time that summer was spent meditating and hiding out in the family room searching Craigslist for apartments. It was a dream, a fantasy but there was no harm in just looking. I imagined myself in the "lovely, light-filled" apartment for months before I got up the nerve to call.

In class, we listened to meditations, journaled, and shared our experiences and aspects of our lives. I loved this new tribe. They were my sanity and support.

Eventually, I was brave enough to tell them I was looking at an apartment. Saying it out loud made it real. I rented the apartment but it took weeks before I was brave enough to tell Jeff. All I could say was that I needed my own space to work things out. I didn't want a divorce. Jeff was devastated. As much as we fought, I'm not sure he thought I would really leave.

What was I doing? What was I doing to Jeff? I felt guilty, numb and scared. I was conflicted. I was second-guessing everything. I was barely functioning. In my new apartment, I was curled up in a fetal position in bed every night and cried myself to sleep. I started attending Al-Anon.

A few weeks later, I was invited to a spiritual event in Fargo.

There were no arguments with Jeff about going, how far I was driving, how long I would be gone, was it necessary to attend. Nothing. I packed a bag, got in the car, and drove away. Damn, could life be this easy, really?

I loved my new freedom and at the same time, I was still conflicted about my marriage. I was stuck, unable to move forward and filled with guilt. Then, Spirit placed a gift right in front of me. Our meditation assistant, Jenny, told us about her experiences as a professional coach. Spirit had nudged this conversation for my benefit. I adored Jenny and we immediately started working together.

Jenny helped me sort my life. What was important to me in all the parts: professional, spiritual, relationships, physical body, creativity, financial, play, and adventure? What were my intentions for them? Where were my blind spots or how was I getting in the way? Clarity was my gift as these pieces of my life started to come together. Coaching became an essential part of my life and to this day, I have a coach.

Months later, I asked for a divorce. We briefly tried mediation. We both hated the experience. By this time, our anger had subsided and we were able to have a conversation that wasn't reduced to screaming. We agreed to try negotiating our own terms for the divorce. This began our weekly meetings at Starbucks. We discussed expenses, assets, and income, all without emotion. Surprisingly, there was laughter and smiles as we met each week. He wanted to keep the house. I wanted to keep the car. The retirement accounts were split. We came to an agreement on Halloween. We were both surprised at how healing the experience was.

One night, a vision appeared during meditation. Jeff stood in front of me with his hands open. He was handing me my freedom and acknowledged, "We loved each other the best we could. We loved each other in the only way we knew how to love." The vision filled me with love and peace. I was able to forgive both of us for our parts in the failed marriage.

Three years after the divorce, Jeff died of cancer. Now, he comes to me through music, meditation, my thoughts, and through others. His love lifts me up and makes me smile.

The last nine years have been good to me. My life is filled with an abundance of color, adventure, freedom, quality and, most of all, Love.

Pat Mork is a Human Resources executive and executive coach. She has worked at a much beloved family-owned manufacturing company for twenty-five years. Her spiritual journey began fourteen years ago with her first meditation class.

Pat grew up in a variety of small towns in Minnesota and Iowa. She and five Iowa high school friends, the "A's," have continued their annual adventures for thirty-plus years. She has lived in the Minneapolis/St Paul suburbs for more years than she can count.

Pat wants to live in a world of light, color, beauty, quality and kindness, filled with cats, dogs, friends and family. When Pat is not at work, she loves traveling, flea-marketing for mid-century finds, acquiring new colorful art for her home, spending time with family, and loving up her two cats, Merlin and Raj.

morkpat@gmail.com

THE COSMIC FLOW OF PROSPERITY

Janice B. Noehulani

At twenty-four years old, I was a single mother in the middle of a custody battle. I was also about three months behind on rent and not sure how I was going to put food on the table.

At that time, I didn't believe in a God. Growing up was really rough and I couldn't even say the word God, much less think It/She/He was here in support of me. But one day, after yet another negotiation with the utility company so they didn't turn off my service, I thought, *What do I have to lose?*

In sheer desperation, I got on my knees and uttered a plea for help.

"If there is a God out there, show me that there is more to my life than this."

I kid you not – an energy moved through me that I can only call unconditional love. It flooded all my senses, my entire body, with a love and a calm I had never experienced before.

A few minutes later, my phone rang. It was the customer service agent I had just spoken to.

"Ma'am," he said, "You don't have to worry about this anymore. Your bill has been paid in full. Your balance is zero."

"But how?" I asked, confused and doubtful.

"I do not know," he replied, "but it just happened and I just thought you would want to know."

As I write this, I remember the feeling of shock as vividly as if it was yesterday. I am not sure what I said to the agent after that, but I do know that energetically I have since thanked him countless times for his part in that miracle.

It changed my life forever.

That moment, and many after, also set me on my path to help people align with their unique frequencies of Prosperity and Cosmic Flow.

By the way, when I say the word prosperity, I not only mean money, but love, joy, health, and abundance in all its forms. When you align with Cosmic Flow, the things that are meant for you in this life just come. You begin to be at the right place at the right time, the right people show up in your life, your purpose and passions unfold with greater ease, and money flows to you.

But many people have a lot of misconceptions about this.

Often people think that you "arrive" permanently, and feel blissful and healed forever.

But often that is not the case.

The journey of spiritual, vibrational alignment, and getting to Cosmic Flow can be grueling. It is not easy to start shedding all the illusions and narratives that you have taken on or been given. We all have many stories, and though some of them are true, many are rooted in mistruths and misunderstandings, passed down through generations and placed on top of our own personal history that block us from Cosmic Flow.

I know this was the case for me. I have never been known to do things the easy way, and my illusions held a firm grasp on me; therefore, the process of spiritual awakening and aligning with my authentic vibrational frequency has been an intense one.

Honestly, no matter how much work I do and how many miracles I witness daily in my life and my clients' lives, the process, this journey of expanding and awakening, is never done. I'm not alone, though; in fact, anyone actually doing "THE INNER WORK" will tell you the exact same thing.

I have been blessed to work with thousands of people to help them align with their signature frequencies, and the majority of them have the same experience: miracles, shedding, tears, and triumphs.

Sure, there are the few who just effortlessly align, create miracle after miracle and never look back, and I AM Grateful for their ease.

All I know is that whatever your journey looks like, it is a worthwhile one.

Below are a few tasty treats to help you align with your prosperity vibration, but first I have something to say about money. Money is *sooo* misunderstood and abused. And, when it is focused upon with the eyes of sacrifice, scarcity and lack, it often retracts.

The next statement may trigger people BUT IT MUST BE SAID:

Not everyone is supposed to have millions of dollars. Not everyone is supposed to be rich.

Karma often dictates it so.

If you were abusive with money or power in a previous lifetime and have the potential to be abusive with money and power in this lifetime, your soul will attempt to sway you at every turn – and that is the way your soul is loving and respecting you.

However, if you are meant to give to humanity, and in order to do that you need five million dollars, you will receive it, so long as you keep your focus on the giving rather than the money itself.

This is just one example, but does it make sense?

Your embodied soul, will, and ego will protect you at all costs from doing damage.

Now, it is possible to change your karma – to dissolve it and transform it. It's quite easy, actually, but that is information for another time.

Simply put, manifesting money is natural to some but not everyone, but that does not mean you cannot experience prosperity and abundance. I am not a money manifester, and yet I never worry about it. It flows in plenty. My attention is on sharing my gifts of empowerment with the world and when I do that prosperity flows.

As I write this, I breathe in gratitude and breathe out gratitude.

So let us start there.

Tasty Treat Number One: Gratitude is the Doorway to Cosmic Flow

What gratitude can you awaken in your body right now? Close your eyes and say out loud, "I breathe in gratitude for _____ (fill in the blank) and breathe out gratitude for _____ (fill in the blank)."

Doesn't that feel good?

Repeat the above statement as many times as is helpful before continuing.

I have a lot to say about gratitude, honey.

First, sometimes we gotta fake it. Sometimes, all I can do is be grateful for the fact that I woke up. Can you feel me?

I am not the happy-go-lucky, everything-is-bliss type of healer.

Sometimes, you gotta speak gratitude for that awful and ugly recurring painful thought, thing, or person that keeps arising because it is there to change you. And sometimes, in my statements of gratitude, there are many cuss words. I'm known for keeping it real.

Tasty Treat Number Two: Creation Starts with Imagination

Think about it – everything, from the chair you're sitting on to the paper in this book, began in someone's imagination.

Now, I am going to ask you to work with your imagination to help you align with your creations.

Imagination comes in unique ways to every person. Many people need to move, run, or walk to spur ideas. Others need to record their voice or have sex to get the imagination pumping!

I have an incredible imagination, but for the life of me I cannot do art projects with my friends (they actually laugh at me about it) during their Sunday craft parties! I ACTUALLY HATE IT – and that's okay. It's just not how I imagine or create, and I honor that about myself.

So, how does your imagination and creation move through you? If using your imagination doesn't come easily, start by getting curious. Do you connect to your imagination through sound, words, dance, art, song, visions, meditations, written word, movement...?

You can also ask yourself how you imagined when you were a child. Did it come through stories? Through fantasy? Just play, my dear. Get curious. Bring that childlike wonder to how your imagination and creations show themselves to you.

As you get more comfortable with this you will see how you get better at co-creating with the Universe.

Tasty Treat Number Three

Next, read this exercise straight through and then DO the exercise. You ready? Great!

I want you to use your imagination and ask your body what "No" looks, sounds, or feels like.

What answer did you get? It can come in many ways – as a color, shape, a feeling or movement in your body, or knowing in your being. Just go with the immediate thing that shows itself to you.

Now I want you to do the same thing with the word "YES."

What answer did you get?

Next ask, "What do I desire? What would fill my heart right now?" Write it down. Pick the first thing that comes to you. Because this is a book about prosperity, I am going to use prosperity as a desired outcome.

Now, I want you to connect to the molecules and atoms inside your body (or at least one molecule and atom).

This is the cellular structure inside of you. Do you see it? Can you feel it? Can you sense it?

I want you to ask your molecule and atom the following questions. You are only looking for a yes or no answer. Write down what immediately comes to you and leave judgment behind. (That said, I was TOTALLY SURPRISED at the answers I received the first time I did this process!)

"Is prosperity inside of my molecule(s) and atom(s)?"

"Is receiving prosperity safe?"

"Is unconditional love inside of me?"

"Is joy?"

Go slow with each one.

Any answer after three seconds is probably just your mind talking. You want to listen to your intuition and imagination, which is YOUR IMMEDIATE RESPONSE.

If you got a yes as your answers, HALLELUJAH!

Go to the process below.

If you got a no on any of these questions, don't worry... I got ya, babe.

Now, here is the fun part: The Remedy.

Call upon your healing helpers. Your soul will understand this. In the beginning, say it out loud; later you can call upon them quietly. Ask for the helpers who can specifically help with this process. These helpers may be alive, like me, but many will be in spirit form. If you like connecting to your ancestors, ask for the "healed ancestors" to come. Feel their presence and thank them for their grace and support.

If you aren't feeling anything, no problem! Just go with it! Sometimes we just have to have some faith.

No matter what your answers were, do these first two processes.

Ask your helpers to connect you to your life cord. This is a white (sometimes gold or gold and white) light that streams from the heavens. This is ONE element to connect you to your vibrational frequency. It is filled with Divine energies and elements. Ask your helpers to have them stream this down into you from the heavens, filling you, and then root it into the pure heart of the Earth (at the center of the Earth).

Feel free to sit with this loving energy as long as possible.

Next, ask your helpers to bring down from the heavens the frequency, vibration, and energy of unconditional love and fill and surround your molecules and atoms with it.

We start here because doing this first allows you to receive everything else more effortlessly.

How does that make you feel? I personally can sit with this energy all day and night. I LOVE IT.

Next, do the same with joy. We all can use more unconditional love and joy, right?

Then do the remaining in this order:

Download within your molecules and atoms the frequency, energy and vibration of:

Safety, and then Prosperity.

You can do these processes for anything you want to create; however, this is a good place to start to help you ignite Your Cosmic Flow of Prosperity.

These are only a few potent processes to activate your Cosmic Flow.

If you need assistance, please ask for help. We need each other, loves.

But most importantly, remember to enjoy the ride to your unique Cosmic Flow. It will be a Divine Adventure.

Janice B. Noehulani is a natural-born Psychic, Shamanic Love and Life Coach, Spiritual Mentor, Teacher, Author, Mother, Lover of Earth, Animals and Humanity. She has been blessed to work with hundreds of people around the globe bringing Eternal and Ancient Transformational Vibrational tools.

She is a clear bridge between the Etheric worlds and the Physical world.

Janice is known for her contagious laugh and BEING a Motorcycle Riding Spiritual Gangsta who is on a mission to normalize self-healing, empowerment, spirituality and awakening.

She teaches empathic, intuitive people how to hear their own wisdom, live into and increase their gifts, and BE Spiritual Love and Light Warriors.

It is her thought that as we heal ourselves, we have a greater ability to heal our families, communities and the entire world.

Janice is passionate about healing our oceans and bringing awareness about how our daily choices affect the world. YOU ARE MORE POWERFUL THAN YOU THINK.

linktr.ee/JaniceNoehulani

THE FREEDOM OF FEELING IT ALL

Jessica Ott

Life has its different seasons – we've all experienced them. I still have these knowings in my heart that when things don't go as planned, the Universe always provides what I need, when I need it. I can relax and trust that as I calm my nervous system and find what feels good, things will all fall into place. Sometimes I find it so easy to get flustered or frustrated when I attach to events or things that are happening around me. I get caught up in what other people are doing or saying or circumstances that are challenging in my life. I get lost in this brain space and I am blinded by "how things have to happen"; I simply forget that the Universe has infinite ways to bring good and abundance into my life in so many different and unexpected ways that are limitless and beyond my own imagination. It's this great mystery of life that makes it such an adventure.

One of the most important things I've discovered is letting go of attachment to outcome. Let life surprise you! Dream in your mind, but don't hold on so tightly to the "how." The thing you are wanting may be down a different path that is more exciting than anticipated. And for sure there are twists and turns on the journey that bring nuggets of wisdom and information that will provide direction and assistance as you progress along the path.

In my own life I've seen so many instances of this. I left my healthcare job near the end of 2020 with no clue what was next for me. I decided to move out of my cozy apartment and be a nomad for a while, since that time I've had many adventures, throwing me fully and completely into the space of the unknown. It has been both exhilarating and terrifying to just live life one step at a time, trusting that clarity around the next place to stay would come, trusting that the money would come, trusting that support from other humans and from my own higher self would show up when I needed it. On this adventure, I've traveled across the U.S., deepened my connection with my family of origin, and met new friends that feel like soul family. I've also met others with whom I really feel a connection from all corners of the globe! All of this has happened in such an organic way, I feel like a completely different person, someone that I'm starting to really like and enjoy being around! This has, of course, taken time and patience, and I am ever-evolving. Just when I think I know something I realize I actually know nothing! There are still many times when I've tried to force things to happen instead of just relaxing into what wants to come. And it always comes through clearly that this isn't the way anymore.

We are human beings put on this earth to ENJOY life. To have fun and experience it all. Does this mean there won't be hard times? Absolutely not. But the hard times are so raw and real and rich; they can be true gifts if we are open to FEEL and experience the depth of it all. The gift of *feeling it all* is where we find freedom. And when you have that feeling of emotional freedom in your heart and mind, there is an unseen force of good and abundance that wants to come into your life. That wants to bring you everything that your heart desires, effortlessly, without striving or force. That emotional freedom is the key to unblocking the gates or doors to abundance in your life.

In my own journey I've found three practices that allow me to experience more emotional freedom in my everyday life. These are "practices," not rigid perfectionistic rituals, (trust me – as a perfectionist in recovery, I understand), so let go of any rules and expectations that you have. This is about freedom, after all! Freedom in your heart and in your mind brings so much freedom in other areas of our lives as well – if we just let go of the outcome.

The first thing that frees my mind to allow in more new ideas, abundance, and changes in perspective is daily journaling. First thing each morning, I start with writing, by hand, two to three pages (or I set a timer for twenty to thirty minutes) about whatever comes to mind. I let the pen keep moving on the paper and just see what comes up. Every day is different, but it allows my mind to become more clear and open to new ideas and to take on the day with a clean slate. Oftentimes, new ideas might pop in if I ask for guidance. I like to use the question, "What do I most need to know today that will be for the highest benefit to myself and others?" Then I let the pen float across the page and tell me what I need to know. I especially recommend this if you wake up in the morning very anxious or grumpy. It allows your racing mind to slow down a bit and your day will flow better – I promise!

The second thing that has brought me peace, clarity, wisdom, guidance, and more trust in my own intuition is time in nature. It is SO important to spend daily time in nature, especially when you are looking for guidance. Mother Earth has this wonderful way of showing us, through the plants and through the trees, the wisdom of our true selves. Being out in nature reminds us of who we really are, without the filter of societal expectations or demands from other people. The trees have so much wisdom to share. They have such grace and the ultimate ability to go with the flow, to change with the seasons, to surrender to what is, and to just keep going. And if you look around you can see how perfect everything is in nature – just the way it is. And the same is true with you! Mother Nature accepts us and sees us for who we truly are at the core of our being, and reminds us of the beauty of our own authenticity and radiance.

This unconditional love and acceptance she has shown me has been a beautiful reminder of how to become more unconditionally loving and accepting of myself.

When the winds blow, be like a tree and root into the practices that nourish and ground you. The birds, plants, flowers, animals, rocks, winds, rain, sun, and moon can be great teachers if we are willing to go to them, to get quiet and still, and just listen.

You can find beauty and inspiration in nature anyplace you happen to be, even in a city or urban area. While you're outside, look around! See what is actually there and be present to your surroundings. If you have the willingness to slow down, being out in nature teaches you how to be present and connect with your inner wisdom.

The third thing that has allowed me to experience more joy, freedom, and abundance in my life is Emotional Freedom Technique (EFT). EFT is a modality that involves tapping on Chinese acupuncture points (or meridians – lines of energy that run throughout the body) while repeating affirmations and stating how you are really feeling. This allows stuck energy in the body to be released, calms the nervous system, and makes space for mental clarity. EFT has given me a practice to move through challenges in my life and shift my perspective, to allow for new possibilities, to rewire my nervous system to a calmer baseline level of functioning where I become a more receptive vessel, and allow more abundance to come in through new ideas, new perspectives, and new beliefs about myself. It has also allowed me to be able to see clearly the truth of who I really am and what is possible, what I am capable of, and what the Universe wants to show me and give to me!

We live in a very giving, loving, and benevolent Universe that is just waiting for us to open up and allow in abundance of all forms. Feeling emotionally free automatically fosters a new allowing, a new openness, a new space of creation to emerge within us that fosters even more freedom in our lives. The freedom from worry about how our lives will unfold, the freedom to be creative, and the freedom to be our true authentic selves, no matter what is going on around us. It is our birthright to feel emotionally free and open to receive all of the abundance, guidance, wisdom, prosperity, surprises, and magic that are always available. And remember – even when you feel out of alignment or not open, even when you do not have special practices or are "doing" or "being" any certain way, you are ALWAYS loved and you are always worthy to receive all of the good that the Universe has planned for you, simply because you exist.

Jessica Ott is a writer, adventurer, and EFT coach. She has a background in physical therapy, which gives her a unique perspective on the connection between mind and body, including emotional blockages manifesting as physical symptoms. Her own self-healing journey led her to alternative healing modalities and energy medicine – and the discovery that the best medicine is always self-love, time in nature, and authentic connection with others. Jessica loves diving deep to help women re-regulate their nervous systems and facilitate discovery within, uncovering core emotional issues and limiting beliefs that hold them back from being their most empowered and authentic selves. Her vision for a healed world includes space for all humans to be free to be themselves and shine their own unique gifts and abilities. When one person shines, it makes it safe for others to shine and a ripple effect is created, fostering a sense of well-being and connectedness that the world is desperately needing right now. Things that bring her great joy include hiking, biking, swimming, music, rainstorms, coffee, and dancing.

jessicaott.com

PROSPERITY OF EXPERIENTIAL CONNECTION: LIVING LIFE IN PURPOSEFUL FLOW

Lizbeth Rizzo

Prosperity! What a beautifully loaded concept. The word itself rolls off the tongue with golden sparkles of eternal promise. When I hear the word, I can envision the future. It brings forth a sense of timelessness. Not fleetingly limited, but expansive. What does it mean to live a prosperous life? The concept of prosperity can be defined with words like abundance, financial stability, wealth, success, and opulence…to name a few. It can often be equated to "things": houses, cars, boats, money, jewels – the richer, finer things in life. What of the "richness" of the *experience of life* – connections to family and friends, mutual respect, empathic support, kind gestures, shared community, divine guidance, special moments/memories, reflective gratitude, blessings, and a sense of wholeness? The *connections* we make and the *experiences* we allow into our lives add a multidimensional quality and richness that, in my opinion, open us to the prosperous and purposeful life paths we are meant to live.

How does one go about creating a life of prosperity? That can depend on perspective and personal attitude. It can be as simple as recognizing and internalizing gratitude for the moments that make up your life and how they fit into your very own grand puzzle…for we each have our own unique purpose here on Planet Earth. Living a life that honors that purpose can look like placing your pieces onto a vast canvas one at a time and watching with awe at how they come together. Each piece is a valued component of experiential prosperity. One blessing at a time. One family/friend connection at a time. One lover at a time. One child at a time. One job at a time. Sometimes it takes a lifetime to understand and recognize the treasures we have received over time (hindsight being 20/20 and all). As a professional social worker, clinical hypnotherapist, past life regressionist, reiki master and energetic healer, I have witnessed individuals internalize feelings of lack, unable to recognize their own self-worth and the value of the amazing lives they have woven together, due to their own limiting beliefs about prosperity… believing that "things" are what define success. I have also seen many individuals over the years connect their prosperity dots through multiple lifetimes, piecing together experiences and internal scripts they hold about it. It can be important to recognize what those scripts are, how they affect manifestation of true prosperity and how to create new connections that lead to our highest good in this lifetime.

I have raised four children, now all young adults and I have witnessed how they came into this world with a level of knowledge of abundant and connected living that has kept me continually adjusting and recalibrating my own ego response based on my cultural conditioning. They get it. Sometimes my own scripts get in their way. I have lived in the United States and abroad, in small towns and big cities, with each life adventure carrying the energy of experiential connection. Living, loving, learning in each place is a piece of my own prosperity puzzle. At times I reflect back on the reasons that I have moved to new locations: sometimes for education, sometimes for employment, sometimes for family. My kids joke that I'm a gypsy. My family says I have *piede lunghi,* an Italian phrase that literally means "long feet" but colloquially describes someone who likes to travel far and away. Ha! Not untrue. My answer always comes back to actively living a Spirit-led life. I go where I am called, and I am blessed and eternally grateful that I have been able to answer my callings in due time. Though, plagued by practicality, I sometimes ask my Angels, are you sure? I question. I drag my feet when it seems unrealistic, too emotionally overwhelming, challenging, et cetera. But I'm a dreamer and when directions come from the ancestors, I listen.

The experience is the important factor. It is *in* the experience that prosperity is found, in the connections with others that are formed. Each move provided experiences profoundly relevant to what my soul needed in that moment to add to my personal prosperity, my personal collection of soul-growth moments. I am first-generation Sicilian and show up with an unseen gaggle of ancestors that whisper what I need to know in any given moment. That's part of our secret. The collective "our." We all have angels, guides and ancestors whispering to us daily, helping us lead our most prosperous life. Can you hear them? Do you trust them enough to act on what you hear? To live a truly uniquely prosperous life that honors your personal life purpose, one must be willing to let go of ego and how you think your life "should" be. The secret is in the listening and allowing yourself to be guided by Spirit and your Inner Knowing/Remembering.

Let me tell you a quick story about letting go. My youngest son was working a part-time job that was not exactly what he wanted to do, but he knew it was a steppingstone that would lead him to something better. He enjoyed the job until the workplace became slightly stressful and he felt undervalued. He was faced with a decision to complete his commitment to the project or stand up for himself. His work ethic dictated that he should ride it out. His commitment to his colleagues and desire to keep his paycheck were stronger than his need to walk away. The day he felt a stronger need to stand up for himself, he decided to leave – without a back-up plan. The day he resigned he sent me a message: "The Universe be sending messages in weird ways." Attached to a screenshot of a job offer with a production company in LA. Better job. His desired location. For people who valued his work. That's how the Universe works, love! The minute he let go of what he thought he "should" do, a more prosperous option manifested.

Ram Das wrote a book many years ago called *How Can I Help?* It speaks of community, sharing resources, love of humanity, being helpful. Sharing is an energetic exchange. We create prosperous flow when we actively share. This is my life path. The Helping and Healing professions are a natural extension of who I AM. The immense blessing of this "knowing" is prosperity. I remember, as a young adult, my family questioning my career choice. The script was, "Social workers don't make any money, how are you going to live?" Money didn't matter to me. Living simply and helping others mattered. I felt connected and attuned to what others were experiencing. I couldn't imagine doing anything else. Of course, having enough money to live matters, and when we allow ourselves to follow what we know in our heart is correct for us, the blessing of connecting to Source and living in the flow is the result. Times when I did NOT follow my own heart and instead listened to what others thought I "should" do, the negative repercussions that followed were tremendously painful. Feelings of immeasurable loss. No flow. Limited connection to Source. It takes conscious effort to come back to center and balance. In this, there is a learning. We are not perfect. We make choices that may ultimately lead us away from being in prosperous flow, but we always have the ability to recalibrate and find balance along our journey.

Why do we consciously make choices that take us out of our own personal prosperity? Usually, it's fear. Fear of what others think. Fear of going against familial expectations/opinions. Fear of the unknown. Fear of making mistakes. I believe there are no "mistakes" in life. Our choices can bring us closer to connection and purposeful living or farther away from connection and our intended prosperity. Living in prosperous experience can seem unattainable when we continually ignore our own intuition and divine guidance by making choices that feed the fear and do not honor what we know in our heart to be our next best step for our highest good. But, if we can recognize the lesson itself as a prosperous moment, it adds value and wisdom to our life experience.

Creating a prosperous life based on experiential connection – completely doable! Here are some ways:

- Ask and you shall receive! Be specific. The Universe has a sense of humor.

- Pay attention! Commit, with heart and soul, to remain open to messages, signs, connections, dreams, intuitive nudges, gut reactions, goosebumps. Actively pursue ways to connect with Source. Meditate. Take walks in nature. Listen to music. Connect with kids and actively listen. They are angels of light and wise beyond their years.

- When you recognize a sign or receive a message, bring it into your heart and love it! It can be easy to continue with your busy day and forget that beautiful moment. When you notice synchronicities, sit with them. Feel them. Honor them.

- Write/Journal. When we write thoughts and messages out, the process of doing so helps us concretize the message.

- Keep a journal near where you sleep so you can write down dreams when details are fresh.
- Show gratitude. Say thank you to your guides, angels, ancestors, for family, friends and earth angels that add value to your life experience.

- Acknowledge the greater purpose this serves. If you are not sure, ask, "What does this mean for me? How will this add value to my life?" Be open to more messages.

- Breathe! Receiving incoming downloads that may require effort to execute can be daunting and downright scary. See the wonder in it all. Lean in. In the words of Thich Nhat Hanh:

    > When you breathe in, your mind comes back to your body, and then you become fully aware that you're alive, that you are a miracle and everything you touch could be a miracle – Everything becomes a wonder.

- Envision/ask: "What will it take… to follow this sign, this nudge, this message; to manifest and accomplish this next step on my prosperous path. What might this mean for my family if I take this next step? Is this in everyone's ultimate highest good?"

- Do it! Make it happen. Create community. Volunteer. Share garden harvests. Say yes to new experiences that add prosperous moments to your life!

Standing witness to the many lives of those who have entrusted their process with me has been a humbling journey of discovery. It helps me fulfill my own life purpose and prosperity. Prosperity is not an end-goal to be acquired. Prosperity is to be recognized for how it presents itself in life's moments. The gift of living IS the prosperous adventure! Bask in the rays of your human, animal and spiritual connections, your experiences, and your loves. For these magical moments are what make up a prosperous life.

Lizbeth Rizzo is a social worker, clinical hypnotherapist, Reiki Master, holistic health coach, author, mother, tree-hugger and social activist. She holds a Bachelor's in Social Work and a Master's in Peace and Justice Studies and is pursuing her PhD in Human Services, as well as certifications in Clinical Aromatherapy and Functional Nutrition. She is certified in various holistic healing modalities including energetic medicine, conflict mediation, and domestic violence trauma and prevention.

Lizbeth intuitively combines modalities for a Mind, Body, Spirit holistic approach to personal and community wellness. Lizbeth holds special interest in past life regression, fascinated by the connective influence of past life experiences in our current reality. She is committed to addressing issues of social justice in our communities, with a special focus on individuals /families experiencing trauma related to domestic violence, trafficking, and homelessness.

Lizbeth currently lives in New Jersey, running her private practice, Angelspace Therapies, and fueling her passion for social justice by working in Social Services with an international human service agency.

AngelspaceTherapies.com

WHEEL OF PROSPERITY
Heidi Royter

Prosperity. Through this process I found myself having difficulty connecting with the word and what it means to me. In the beginning the idea of it made me uncomfortable, something that I could not resonate with, or allow myself to. I sat and thought about my childhood in search of this part of my being and could not find it at first. What I did find from my childhood was the strong ethic and the belief that I could achieve anything I set my mind to. Was this, I wondered, how you become prosperous?

I turned to the internet and to the dictionaries and found that most people define being prosperous as being financially successful. This did not sit well with me because I felt there had to be more to being prosperous than economic well-being. I sat with myself and questioned why our society creates a vision that prosperity is all about money. I have always felt that if you have a roof over your head, clothes on your back, food on the table, and your loved ones around you, this was enough – and that you can conquer and do anything with love. Then I realized I was avoiding something deeper.

I questioned myself again, this time asking what I was afraid of, why I was creating this wall around the thought and feelings of me being prosperous. Why I was not allowing this word to resonate with me? I recognized a discomfort with letting myself flourish and being seen; I had fear around accepting my riches and what people would think. What was this fear all about, where was it coming from and why was it causing me so much uneasiness?

As I began digging deeper into the thoughts, feelings, and emotions running through my being, I realized I did not allow myself to celebrate my successes and receive being prosperous because it felt so foreign to me. I initially was thinking and feeling that I was not taught to celebrate "me," and that others might even judge me for doing so. Clearly, I needed to let these thoughts and feelings go. So what if they did judge me? What did I believe would happen, that they would not be accepting of me? If they were not accepting of me and judging me, then the truth was they should not be in my life anyway. This was simple for me to find my way through, but there was more to explore.

I went back to my childhood. I was taught you had to work hard if you wanted things to be less of a struggle. Everything appeared to revolve around demanding work so I could make a better life, have better opportunities, and do better than my parents.

I did not see my parents regularly celebrate their successes or take a moment to enjoy them. I think they were focusing so hard on creating and providing for the family that they didn't take the time to acknowledge their prosperity. Or if they did, they did so in a way I didn't notice. The work was their celebration – the ability to provide a roof over our heads, clothes on our backs and food in our bellies. Taking trips to California for business and pleasure, and playing at the beach, were also markers of prosperity for my parents.

As I went through this journey, I realized being prosperous is exactly what my parents wanted for me and my siblings. They showed me to work hard to provide for yourself and to enjoy the "little" things. My parents wanted us to have a good, comfortable life, be financially stable and have loving relationships. They did this for us by creating a successful business and giving us what we needed, and taking us on adventures that I had forgotten until now. I also now understand that over the years I had focused on what my parents had sacrificed for me, which had led to feelings that it was wrong to thrive and experience joy and abundance. I also realize I had placed so much of my value on working hard – this was how I had internalized the message that I could do anything I set my mind to.

As I allowed myself to start to connect to the feeling of being prosperous, there was one last bit of resistance, preventing me from stepping into it completely. Those little thoughts and feelings of self-doubt and unworthiness were popping up, that familiar discomfort and fear of what others would think of me. I took a breath and let it go, saying, "I will allow myself to cultivate and receive my successes." I also began to work through these feelings by using the Wheel of Prosperity, focusing on my personal medicine. These are actions I take to bring me to clarity and reclaim something within me when I get lost, disconnected, and ungrounded. This process also supports me in releasing limiting beliefs.

You can create a wheel about anything in life – relationships, health and, as in this case, prosperity. In the Wheel of Prosperity, I reflected on my life and looked at my abundance with family and friends, money, health, my physical environment, the fun I have and recreation activities I participate in, my career, my life purpose, romance and intimacy, and my spiritual alignment. These are what I celebrate.

My prosperity is my inner peace – the security and foundation of who I am, my wholeness, grounded into the earth and connected to the heavens above. Knowing that GOD has a plan and I am surrounded by that love daily. Knowing my nanny, who left this earth when I was a toddler, has been one of my guiding angels through my journey to wholeness, along with my other spirit guides in heaven and on earth, always by my side, cheering me on, pushing me forward, keeping me safe to lead me back to my wholeness.

My prosperity is having a loving and supportive husband, who is my best friend and confidant, being a mother to four amazing children and blessed with two grandchildren and a wonderful daughter-in-law, and to have my parents, siblings, and in-laws around. It is having a mother and father who showed me how to be strong, work hard and love deep. It is having survived countless attempts of self-sabotage and abuse; it is being lost and then finding myself. It is sitting in my backyard with the sun on my face, watching my fur babies run around and hearing the birds chirping all around me. This is prosperity to me and I receive it and celebrate it all. I am thankful for all my experiences, lessons learned, and the work I have done to create the prosperous life I live.

We all deserve to celebrate what we define as our successes. What is your personal medicine, self-care, strategies that have meaning, and purpose in life that makes you feel that you are thriving? I invite you to take actions or acknowledge the actions that you take each day that make you feel good and fulfilled. Celebrate these actions and always remember that all the little things count. Embody this knowing and ground it into your being.

I have learned that life can knock me down, and I can get back up and I can make things happen. Rather than being consumed any longer by old thoughts, experiences, or beliefs, I have chosen to work to transform myself into the person I am today and live the successful life I live today. This is an area of my life I needed to embrace, and this writing experience allowed me to do this, and to connect with what prosperity means to me, in and from my heart.

My hope is for you to explore, expand, and give yourself permission to thrive, be abundant, and be in your wholeness. How you define prosperity is unique to you, just always remember that you were born to be prosperous.

Wheel of Prosperity Journaling Exercise: Take a moment to sit down with a journal, a piece of paper and a pen. You can even use a variety of colored markers, pencils crayons. Just make it personal to you.

- Make a large circle on the paper, with eight sections inside it, like a wagon wheel or like a pie.

- On the inside of each section, name them as follows (if a title does not resonate with you, use what does):
    - Family and Friends
    - Money
    - Health
    - Physical environment
    - Fun and Recreation Activities
    - Career and Life purpose
    - Romance and Intimacy
    - Spiritual alignment

- Center yourself and be open to the magical awareness of self. Look at the sections you have written down. Which one stands out to you? That's where you start.

- Remember to have no judgment or attachment to what arises. This is your unique and personal experience, according to how you define your prosperity.

- Here are some questions to ask yourself:
    - What are my accomplishments?
    - What success have I had that I am not acknowledging?
    - Am I afraid of being prosperous? If so, what am I afraid of? What happens because I am afraid? And what if I continue to believe this way about prosperity? What if I receive it instead?
    - How do I, or can I, celebrate my abundance?
    - What are some words of affirmation I can tell myself?
    - What do I do to give myself quality time and how does it make me feel when I do these things?
    - What acts of service do I perform and why?
    - How do I feel when I am at peace?

- Live well, be magical and prosperous!

Heidi Royter is a COO in the long-term care industry, engagement coach, business consultant, and owner of Be Free Wellness and Yoga. She studied business management at the University of Las Vegas and is a certified Mind-Body Wellness practitioner, which includes life coaching, clinical hypnotherapy, and holistic nutrition. Heidi is also a Unity Yoga practitioner with an additional certification in Yoga Nidra. She is currently in the process of obtaining her associate degree in Mind-Body Transformational Psychology at Southwest Institute of Healing Arts.

Heidi's approach to working with private clients, team members, and businesses is nurturing, spirited, and direct. She uses her education and life experiences to ensure individuals are seen, valued, and heard and can create a strong foundation personally and professionally.

She is also a proud mother, Mimi to her grandchildren, and has been married to her husband and best friend for almost thirty years. In her spare time, she enjoys being in the outdoors, spending time with family, reading, and making jewelry and essential oil blends.

heidi@befreewellnessandyoga.com

LIVING A FULFILLED LIFE
GG Rush

When most people think of prosperity they think of riches, money, a large bank account, being financially free. Those things are all correct, but for me prosperity is something more. Prosperity is the feeling that you are fulfilled in your life and dreams. For example, being a contributing author in *The Wild Woman's Book of Shadows* was a dream come true for me. Being in the company of the "Wild Women" tribe of sisters made me feel wonderfully honored and accomplished. Fulfilled. It is with the same gratitude and pride that I feel in being part of this book and among these incredible Wild Women as well.

What does it mean to feel fulfilled? It means that I am, right this very moment, doing something I love. Fulfillment comes from doing what you are called to do with your life. Success isn't even a necessity; it's certainly rewarding but it isn't the point of the fulfillment. For me, it is the accomplishment of reading my words in print, seeing my name in the table of contents. It is also the feeling of blessing and well- being that makes it fulfilling.

Being fulfilled is being fully satisfied with your life. Being of service is a way to achieve fulfillment. Doing things to help others, supporting your friends and family in their own endeavors and bringing them their own fulfillment. Prosperity and fulfillment bring joy and contentment to everyone's lives. Where can you find your own fulfillment? You can find it inside your heart and your soul. Find your authentic self and your true calling in life and you will live a fulfilled life.

In my life I have studied life coaching, hypnotherapy, Reiki healing and space clearing, and they have become my future as a new business owner. My dreams of owning my own healing practice have come to fruition. I can now be of service to help others in healing and moving forward in reaching their own goals of fulfillment. I can not only listen to what a client is saying but I can HEAR them and help them to understand what is holding them back. I can use all of the skills I have been taught to bring them to a better place in their lives and, in turn, I am also fulfilling myself. I have been blessed and fortunate enough to have some of the very best teachers and mentors to guide me in claiming my calling.

How did I accomplish this? I studied, I took the classes, and showed up. I wanted to change my life and do work that I felt drawn to. I wanted to make huge changes. Who am I and where was I headed? I was a bookkeeper with a small company that I had zero investment in. I was a divorced mother of two grown daughters. I was going through the motions every day. On the side, however, I was attending seminars and classes and traveling the world. I was writing down the bones of my life. But where was the fullness? The fulfillment? The prosperity? Just like Dorothy in the *Wizard of Oz*, it was with me all along! I just needed to walk that Yellow Brick Road and accept the lessons along the way.

I didn't happen overnight; in fact, it took years. And it took years because I didn't believe in myself. I didn't have the confidence to believe I could make it in the business of service and spirituality. Even though I had the world's best teachers and mentors, and even though I knew deep down inside that I really did have what it takes to do this work, I was afraid to take that leap of faith. Fear, of both failure and of success, held me back. What? Fear of success? Yes! It was the fear that I COULD make this my work but I would have to sacrifice nearly everything to jump off that cliff.

The fact that I had become a published author several times over, which was the most amazing accomplishment I had ever had, didn't give me the confidence to say YES to the life I wanted and dreamed of. I continued to take classes as if the more experience I had the more I would be worthy of the life I wanted. I'm not saying the constant and never-ending learning and knowledge I gained didn't add to my feeling of becoming an "expert," but I still felt unworthy of standing next to my mentors and teachers as an equal.

It took a deep dive into my past to discover what was holding me back. One of my teachers and mentors, Dr. Lisa Thompson (who wrote an awesome chapter for this book), spent one afternoon in a hotel room in Hawaii with me, helping me to reach the breakthrough that would finally allow me to see what my biggest fear was. I had internalized the fear of losing everything and being homeless, which was something I had been told while going through my divorce. Once Lisa unlocked that block, I realized I wasn't homeless, and it wasn't going to happen. As a matter of fact, I was financially secure and had equity in my home! When that block was removed, I was able to begin to imagine the possibilities that I could survive on far less income for a period of time and that would allow me to invest time in creating my spiritual business, I felt a sense of freedom and joy that I hadn't felt in years.

Upon my return to the "real world" I immediately posted my resume on a job-seeking site and within twenty-four hours, got a response and an interview. I then took the very bold step of quitting my very stable job of fourteen years and accepted a part-time position at a much smaller company with far less stress and demand on my time and energy. I am not suggesting doing this is for everyone, but it was the right decision for me. These days, I am able to dedicate time in the mornings to meditate, exercise, write, study, and practice my skills. I have the mental space to workshop ideas and make plans for how to get my business off the ground and be successful.

Another way I feel fulfilled is by helping others in their own businesses and successes, especially women, including my mentors and friends. I sign up for their classes and seminars. It is a win-win; I support them by purchasing their products, books, jewelry, crystals, and art, and I am given the opportunity to enjoy more of their offerings. I have also gifted seminars and books to many of my friends so that they too can discover these mentors and artisans. It is so rewarding when I see friends starting out in businesses and making their mark and becoming fulfilled in their lives!

How can you feel fulfilled in your own life? Start with journaling what it is that you want to do. Are you content in what you are doing every day? Is there more? Seek out people to be your inspiration. They can be local or online. Look at their websites and read their books. Be inspired by their mission statements and form your own. Find your true calling. Experiment. Take classes and seminars. It is all out there for you.

As you can see, prosperity is so much more than money. It can be equated to fulfillment, happiness, contentment, pleasure, and success. You can be in a relationship that brings you fulfillment – be it romantic or platonic. You can be providing a service that helps others to be happy and flourish in their lives. You can set goals and be generous with your time. Be grateful for what you have in your life. Be a role model for young people. Volunteer and mentor others. Create a personal ritual of kindness and generosity. Dive into your spirituality through daily meditation. Discover new places that bring you peace and joy. Walk in nature and observe the world around you. Read and study to keep your mind active and working.

Take up a craft, draw, paint, take photographs, try a cooking class. I personally love to travel and experience different cultures and food. See the world! We can enjoy those things in our own lives, and we can also share them with others so they achieve prosperity as well.

Growing up, one of my favorite shows was "Star Trek." Looking back, I realize that when Mr. Spock said, "Live long and prosper" I never thought he was referring to money, but to the richness of health, openness, and joy. So go out and live a fulfilled life full of prosperity and happiness. Be the person you were meant to be!

Gail "GG" Rush Gould is an author, certified life coach, clinical hypnotherapist and clutter clearing coach. She is a certified Reiki Master and has studied aromatherapy, chakra balancing, toxic emotions and the ancient art of pulse reading. She has traveled the world solo and will continue her journey to see the world and find herself. GG resides in Cary, North Carolina with her cat Bella.

gg-rush.com

SURRENDER AND ALLOW AND THE UNIVERSE WILL RESPOND

Betty Skinner

"Prosperity ~ a way of living and thinking, not just having more money and things. A prosperous life must include joy and happiness, a healthy body, and personal relationship with Spirit. It is not just a monetary goal."

–Anonymous

We have all heard about manifesting and prosperity, yet we wonder how it seems to just "magically" happen for a few. For the majority, manifesting seems to always be just outside of one's reach. They wonder and worry why they can't just produce the miracles they need, when they need them. I used to be among that majority… until I was guided to the missing connection via a Divine moment of you-just-can't-make-this-stuff-up. I learned that you need to let go of "control" in order to ALLOW. That is when the Universal Blessings appear (by Divine Universal timing), You can't allow if you are still demanding to have control (your time, your way).

"Surrender" is not, as many people assume, a form of weakness, but liberation from attachment. To surrender means you remove your limitations. We tend to want to control our outcomes because our brain is hardwired for certainty. Control means to overanalyze a situation until you are drained. When I looked at it from this angle, I realized this doesn't leave much room for the energy of prosperity and magic. That was the piece that was missing from my "manifesting" life. In order to ALLOW the magic & miracles, I had to let go of my tight grip on control. Of course, I had to experience this firsthand to learn how it works.

I had spent thirty-plus years in the insurance industry, and over the course of that time the awareness that something was "off" and that I wasn't in my soul alignment started to get louder and louder. While I loved my clients and community partnerships, I was growing more and more sensitive to the misalignment of the corporation processes. I realized I wasn't living life to the fullest and was just existing.

The pain of the realization that I could not continue in the industry came after I experienced a life implosion that took me to a very "dark night of the soul." Little did I know at the time that going down that rabbit hole would lead me to a spiritual healing journey that changed my life. In that time of deep, dark depths of despair I contemplated checking out of this journey called life. My connection to the Angels that I had experienced lightly up until that time was the reason I'm still here. But it was the extreme darkness that led me to search for the "light." And during that search I discovered my career was draining my soul.

How was I going to change my career path? I had run a successful agency in my community on my own for over twenty years. Some of my clients I had worked with for more than three decades and were like family. How was I going to quit on them? Also, how was I going to give up the only thing I knew how to do? It was all I had. How could I let it go? As the process of doing so started to emerge, I entered another state of fear and lack and uncertainty. I became extremely stressed and agitated about what would happen with my agency and my clients if I left. The more I worried and stressed, the more I tightened my grip.

After many, many months of sleepless nights and health concerns, I turned in my resignation on the summer solstice of 2020. The sun has always had a special connection to my heart and Spirit, and I found it comforting to know I would start the unwinding process on such a Divine energetic day. Shortly after I submitted my ninety-day notice of resignation, another agent in town put in a request to corporate to purchase my office. Unfortunately, corporate denied the request, and my hands were tied as to what I could disclose to my clients and community partners. Basically, this meant I couldn't tell them I was leaving, which only increased my stress and worry. It took months of trying to clear out and close out all remaining service needs for my clients. Now this is where I insert my prior mention of "you just can't make this stuff up."

I was in the office on a Saturday (at this point I was working seven days a week to prepare for closing the office). I had just finished a detailed email to a commercial client about her upcoming insurance renewal. My instructions to her were to fill out her renewal questionnaire form and return it to me prior to her upcoming renewal. After I hit "send," the finality and reality hit me. And it hit me HARD! It was a moment of realization that by the time she returned her renewal questionnaire, I was going to be gone and my email would no longer be valid. If her renewal was not processed in time, her insurance could be canceled, which meant her husband, a general contractor, would have his business license suspended. The stress and worry in that moment sent me to my knees and uncontrollable sobbing from my mouth. I think I said a prayer to my Angels to help me through this (and to release control), then crawled back into my chair.

The very next email to answer was from an email address I had never seen before. The username: AngelWing! This grabbed my attention because I have always had a special connection to Angels and an incredibly special Angel Team that always Divinely supported me when needed.

Turns out it belonged to a client that I had been honored to serve for my entire agency career. He was an elderly gentleman who always called or stopped in, so I had never seen his special email address before. His email was just a response to a corporate survey, but I heard a voice say, "Call him" behind my right ear. This is usually a sign of Divine intervention when I "hear" a voice behind my right ear. And it wouldn't stop. I heard, "Call him, call him, call him," several times. I immediately went into panic mode, thinking something had happened to him. I nervously picked up the phone to dial his number and felt even more panic when his wife (who I had never spoken to in all these years) answered. I was extremely relieved to hear her say he was at the store.

Then, still sniffling from my emotional breakdown a few moments before, I told her my real reason for calling was to ask how he had come up with his email address. She proceeded to tell me the sweetest story of how he collected lighthouses all his life and she collected Angels. When the time came for him to establish an email address, he was frustrated that using the word "lighthouse" was too long, so she suggested using "angel" instead.

By the time she finished telling me the story, I was crying so hard I could not speak. She asked if I was okay, and I managed to clear my throat and let her know about the stress that I was under in trying to make a HUGE shift in my life. What she did not know as she so sweetly told me about their collections of lighthouses and angels, was that I had already been forming a new side business of intuitive energy healing work, which had been my passion for helping others since my "dark night of the soul" experience. But what was most incredible was the name of my new business, for which I had created a Facebook page a year earlier: ANGEL LIGHTHOUSE!

She gave me the beautiful advice that I needed to move forward with my new path. I ended the call to find I was able to take a DEEP breath. It felt like it was the first time I could BREATHE in months! Two weeks later, I received a phone call from the agent that had tried to purchase my office a few months back, saying that he wanted to submit another request. I agreed to let him do so, believing that corporate would just deny him again, but I would have more time to wrap up the office. After my phone call with my elderly client, I had already "let go" of the control. I had surrendered. I was allowing whatever to be, to be. I knew my Angels and the Universe would have my back after the sweet client interaction of Angel Lighthouse. I proceeded in preparation to shut down my office and move forward on my new life path.

A few weeks later the call came that the agent was indeed APPROVED to take over my agency! It was synchronicity at its finest, and confirmation after I had surrendered and let go of control and resistance. I knew at that Divine moment that the Universe truly did have my back. When you surrender and let go of control to ALLOW, the energy of prosperity flows freely. The beautiful energy of prosperity now means magic and miracles every day. Some big, some small. Living in balance and harmony. Living in peace. Living connected to soul. Living in an ongoing state of success that touches every area of our lives. That, to me, is prosperity.

Betty Skinner has recently spent time unwinding from her corporate career, in which she received multiple community awards, and is currently redesigning her life path. Betty has a lifelong passion, which for thirty years manifested as coaching insurance clients, is now fueling her transition into intuitive energy healing. To this end, she has been training and studying and integrating several modalities (to process her own personal healings) and will now be assisting clients in their own self-empowerment.

Betty is a lifelong student of personal development. Her unique trainings, certifications, and research include hypnotherapy, channeling, intuitive healer, chakra clearings, soul entrainment, Akashic Records, guided meditations, alchemy, sensitive empath guidance, theta healing, and others.

Her personal interests are travel, music, resort spa trips for self-care, road trips, painting, and reading. Her favorite time is any time spent on the ocean, and she has a dream to have a beach house someday. Betty resides in the beautiful Pacific Northwest.

Angel–Lighthouse.com

ALTAR & SEX MAGICK

Rachel Srinivasan

For me, feeling prosperous and abundant has been a long and winding journey, one that has had its share of struggles. At the ripe young age of one and a half I began to draw and have been an artist ever since. I studied art and was unfortunately repeatedly fed programming about "starving artists." Even close family didn't approve of my career choice. Coupled with this, I became a mother during my second year of college, choosing to start a family earlier than anticipated. Young and ill-equipped for motherhood, I quickly fell into depression, all the while dependent on food stamps and various government programs.

These early years were stiflingly difficult, centered around stress and heartbreak. Prosperity was the last thing on my mind – I just wanted to survive to the next semester and graduate! Knowing things needed to change, I decided I needed to learn more about myself. Since then I have uncovered the mysteries of being a woman, and have developed a strong relationship with the spirit realm. At times it has been a lonesome process, but as I stepped into ever-increasing self-acceptance I have embraced the mysterious and unseen, including sacred space and my body's energy. Learning about who I am, not who others think I am or who my family tells me to be, is a very important element of feeling prosperous.

I'm from Omaha, Nebraska, in the heartland of America and its geographic center. Though I'm very grateful for my midwestern roots, it has taken a long time to figure out that I do not need my family's approval to move forward on my journey. I'm a psychic medium, specializing in spirit art, tarot card reading, and Reiki healing, and have been giving readings and healings professionally for about three years. Before that, I worked in digital marketing, and I'm a bestselling author. Yet, though I wear many hats, I still don't have it all figured out. As a business owner, I don't always feel prosperous; in fact, I often feel as though I am at the mercy of some mysterious force in the Universe. What I have come to realize is that while this is true in some respects, that mysterious force in the Universe is actually me. I am powerful. I'm going to share a few practices that I use to harness that power and bring abundance into my life. These two useful tools are altars and sex magick.

It's important for me to feel highly connected to Spirit while I am working and in my private life, therefore, I make my home into a comfortable and luscious living space. One practical way of connecting to Spirit is through an altar. The altar is a both ancient and modern spiritual symbol of what is important for you. My altar is a lovely, light pink curio cabinet table. It's clear to see by looking at it that I am a crystal grid and essential oil enthusiast. There are also platonic solids (a category of geometric shapes), seashells, prayers, and a pendulum.

Many wild women have altars and if you don't I highly recommend setting one up. Altars can be any size, on bookshelves, tables or desks. They can be dedicated to a number of different things, or to their creator by default. They often contain bowls, candles, amulets, crystals, herbs, pictures, plants, and any other cherished objects. Take mine, for example: I have a crystal grid. I enjoy candles. There are tarot and oracle cards too. An altar is also a form of communication – a bridge to Spirit – and in my case, the Norse goddess Freya, as I am currently working with rune magic.

Other altars may have unique altar cloths, symbols for the elements. The tree of life, plants, flowers, photos of ancestors and representations of Jesus, Mary, Buddha, and angels are all common, as are symbols of the sun and moon and male and female energies. Here is a list of common components:

1. The air element: a feather, bird, or swords tarot card
2. The water element: a vessel filled with water, seashells, any water deity, cups tarot card
3. The fire element: a pyramid, candles, an image of a flame, wands tarot card
4. The earth element: soil, food, coins, money, jewelry, or a pentacles tarot card
5. Something beautiful beloved by the altar owner
6. A deity or a picture of a revered family member

If nothing in the above list resonates, then simply use items based on your own inclinations.

Another tool that I use to feel prosperous is sex magick. This might seem taboo, but it's actually a simple and very ancient form of magick still common today. Every wild woman uses different modalities to work with energy, consciously or not, and every writer of this book has pushed the boundaries in some form or fashion. Besides, engaging in sexual activity is not pushing the boundaries, but a natural part of the human experience.

The first thing to know is that sex magick is about understanding yourself – understanding your body and what is important to you. What's a goal regarding abundance? Write about it, envision it, fantasize about it, and create a mantra for the altar. The major premise of sex magic is the power and importance of human sexual energy. When sexual creative life-force energy is released in the form of an orgasm, it is one of the most forceful forms of energy a human can make, if not the most powerful of all. I also recommend having an altar for sex magick, as part of the ritual. It's a way to believe where the energy or goals are held, especially if the goals or requested energy is written out and then the written note placed on the altar.

Intention is everything when it comes to spiritual work. Sex magick does not require a partner, but if one is involved they should be on the same page with the wild woman. They also must be trustworthy, supportive, and make her feel safe. Here are the main steps in practicing sex magick.

Step one is creating a sacred space. This can be as simple as lighting a few candles, meditating, or having special music playing. Setting the mood is important. Is there anything that should be placed on the altar to represent the sacredness of the event? Make sure to prepare the space beforehand.

Step two is visualizing the goal. Visualization is a key component to this type of magick. Meditation helps with visualization. Perhaps a vision board has been created already. Visualize money, gold, or a calendar full of profitable events and bookings. How does it feel to reach your goal? What would it feel like in your life if the goal would be achieved? Try to visualize and feel every single part of the goal. Have an extremely clear picture in your mind's eye.

Step three is to engage in the sex act itself! Again, a partner is great but not required. Solo practitioners are just as successful as anyone else. Just enjoy yourself while also visualizing the goal being attained at this time. A key component in this step is trusting and enjoying the moment or enjoying your partner. For the wild woman, the end goal can be visualized during this step. Imagine what the goal will feel like and how lovely that sensation is. For the wild woman, as long as the envisioned goal is involved here during sex, the magick is activated.

Step four is to reach climax and release this strong creative force into the Universe. Climaxing is great but not necessarily required for female participants of sex magick. Visualizing the goal during the sex act is enough. For male participants, however, the climax specifically is the stage in which the goal must be envisioned. Otherwise the sex magick is not activated.

Step five is to release and let go of the visualization. Give thanks for the experience. Rest and trust in the Universe. Know that your goals are arriving. Don't continue to obsess about your goal; in fact, don't think of it much at all. Just know that what is now yours will come to you soon. If it doesn't arrive in the timely manner, there may be other details and circumstances that might have been outside of your awareness, or the desired goal wasn't meant for you. Trust in the Universe.

Whenever setting intentions or creating new goals in my life, I incorporate them into my altar. At the time of this writing, I have incorporated runes – which I have created and consecrated from scratch – into my daily magical and spiritual practices. Experiencing and learning about runes has furthered my connection to my Nordic heritage. Runes have their own lore and magic that easily fit into sex magick. The color red was a very important ceremonial color for the Vikings and I have incorporated it. However, if red items aren't available, a color that invokes power and strength would work. During a meditation I was shown some bear-shaped candle sticks. The next day I searched for them, not finding anything that would match my vision. Later I found polar bear candle holders that have worked well. The bear is a symbol of powerful protection and strength, so I know I'm protected when delving into my endeavors.

Sex magick is powerful and easily executed by almost anyone – both solo practitioners and those in supportive partnerships – to attract prosperity and abundance. I have used it to attract a full schedule of clients and a loving partner. Sex is a common theme in the human experience so why not use it in an intentional and spiritual manner?

There are numerous tools at the disposal of a spiritual woman that can bring prosperity and I hope all the wild women readers will explore them for themselves. Learn what you like. Be joyful. Enjoy life. Experiment with creating an altar and adopt the simplest magic, sex magick, into your personal practice. Whatever tools and methodologies you choose, just know that you are worth it. You're worth getting to know your best friend, yourself!

Rachel Srinivasan is a psychic medium, painter, professional spirit artist, and Reiki Master Teacher. Born in Oklahoma, Rachel began drawing at one and a half years old and has never stopped. Her family later moved to Nebraska, where as a high school student she received the Marie Walsh Sharpe Scholarship. She also participated in an exchange program in Rome, where she was immersed in Italian art and language and introduced to oil painting. Upon returning to the U.S., she attended Arizona State University, where she earned two bachelor's degrees, as well as a painting scholarship from the Phoenix Art Museum. After working in digital marketing for ten years, she left the corporate world to focus on her own business. She became a Reiki Master Teacher in 2017 and attended the International Spiritualist Federation and became a professional spirit artist in 2019. Today, Rachel's artwork is exhibited and sold by collectors in Dubai, Turkey, San Francisco, and Phoenix. She lives in Tempe, Arizona with her daughter and loves to surf, paddleboard, and dance.

GrandRisingSpiritual.com

OPENING DOORS TO ABUNDANCE

Cynthia Stoneman

How are you at letting someone open a door for you? A physical door. Do you reach for the door? Or do you let someone open it for you? Opening the door yourself may feel like independence, as in, "I can take care of myself" or even, "I don't need anyone to help me." Well, that energy could be blocking your abundance.

Abundance comes in many forms: new job opportunities, quality time with people you care for, adventures, a beautiful sunset, time to write a book, helpful people, gifts, money and so much more. Everything in our life is energy. We exchange energy daily with everyone and everything we encounter. The more we exchange energy, the more it flows to us, as well as from us. Opening doors is an energy exchange.

Think about the last time someone invited you to lunch. You enjoyed a nice meal, shared new ideas and memories, and listened to each other's recent successes and challenges, sometimes crying and sometimes laughing. So much was shared during this enjoyable event. When the check arrived, did you allow your host to feel the joy of giving to you, or did you reach for your wallet, thus robbing both of you of a blessing? Many of us are very good at giving and uncomfortable with receiving. That creates an imbalance in the energy exchange process.

When there is an imbalance of giving and receiving, there may be a lack of abundance in life. There can be challenging personal relationships with friends, family, coworkers, and partners. A feeling of being stuck and not knowing how to move forward. A feeling that the world is against you. Feeling like bad luck is the only luck you have. I remember being in that space. I was there for a long time. I know a way to change that. Let me open a door for you.

My gift is providing the words people need to hear, when they need to hear them. When people meet me, my sparkly personality gives the impression that I do not have darkness in my life. That I live a charmed life. Well, I do have darkness in my life, just like everyone else in this world. On my darkest day, my first husband called me at work and ended his life while I was on the other end of the line. I know devastation and darkness. I also know I get to choose how I show up each morning. Most days are a balance of dark and light. We need that balance, just like we need balance in giving and receiving. Allowing people to open doors can help with the balance.

In my adult life, I have been on food stamps, government housing, and subsidized daycare for my children. I've stood in line for government surplus food boxes and asked charitable agencies to pay my utilities. I shopped at thrift stores, church rummage sales and yard sales because I couldn't afford more. I am not ashamed of using these services. At the time, I looked at it as a helping hand. I now see it as letting people open doors for me.

Norma opened a big door during that time. She hired me for a full-time job! At my interview she offered to drive me to and from work daily. It was ten miles away, and my husband and I didn't have a car. Two years later, Norma retired, and I moved out of state. When I returned to Arizona, the company rehired me the same day

– and they offered me more money! The doors continued to open. During my ten years there, I was given opportunities to create training manuals, attend college classes, train employees, and learn computer software and hardware. When doors opened, I said yes, not realizing that the Universe was helping me through the baby steps that would create a lifelong passion and career for training and teaching people.

Helpful people are everywhere. Take off the blinders and look at people in a different way – without judgment or expectation. As you practice, it will become second nature to you. Helpful people don't always need a physical door to appear. For instance, being five-foot-three, the top shelf at the grocery store is usually a challenge for me. I close my eyes for a moment and call in a helpful person who can help me get the item from the top shelf. Open my eyes and wait a few moments to see the helpful person arrive. I speak up for my want or need. "Would you help me? I am short and cannot reach the top shelf. I need six of those bottles, please." When they agree, I thank them. I thank the helpful person again after I have the items. The person might be a taller man, or six-foot-tall woman. It may be a clerk with a ladder. The person may not speak my language. I remember to be open to anyone kind enough to assist me, even if they do not appear as I thought they should. I am calling in a helpful person for a small task. In most cases, this does not lead to a lifelong relationship; however, the joy you will feel from giving gratitude and allowing someone to give to you is a lifelong practice.

Everything is energy. The air that we breath. Sand between our toes. Our physical bodies are energy. A family outing is full of all kinds of energy. Food that nourishes our bodies. Furniture, cars and many other material things. Even money is energy. EVERYTHING is energy, and we are simply exchanging it all day, every day.

In time, you will begin to see helpful offers coming to you. Some may seem small and insignificant, but they are great practice for accepting abundance.

- Coupons for discounts or free items. I rarely clip coupons or use electronic coupons; however, I do pay attention when it is something I will use. A free sandwich at my favorite eatery – yes, please! Birthday desserts too. Grocery stores now send custom coupons for frequently purchased items, presenting a great opportunity to stock up.

- Upgrades on flights, rental cars, trains, hotel rooms, et cetera. Ask if there are upgrades. My knight and I took a train ride. Purchased second class on the way to the destination, and coach on the way back. On the ride, we enjoyed walking through all the cars on the train. Coach cars did not look comfortable. At the destination, our first stop was the ticket counter to upgrade to first class. Internet service was not good there. Our helpful person couldn't tell us how much the upgrade charge was. We would find out when we got to the starting station. We trusted the Universe and bought the tickets. At the station, the charge was about fifty dollars for the upgrade for both of us, which was two hundred less than the original first-class tickets.

- Random rebate of refund checks. These are interesting because you never know when one will show up, or how much it will be. Could be a forty-seven-cent dividend check, thirty-five dollars overpaid on a loan three years ago, or thirty thousand in an old retirement account that was forgotten. No matter the size of the check, the energy equivalent is the same. Money energy coming in, gratitude energy sent in return.

- Gifts that seem too good to be true. A client, Marie, loves vacations. She works so she can take vacations and travel. A group of her close friends were going on a Mediterranean cruise. One friend asked Marie to join them as his guest. He had already paid for a second person who could not attend. The money would be wasted if Marie did not attend. Marie thought this gift was too extravagant and she would not be able to pay him back. When she asked my advice, I reminded her that she had asked the Universe for an amazing vacation. The invitation was clearly a gift without strings attached. She knew everyone in the group and they would enjoy her being there. Marie accepted the gift and enjoyed the once-in-a-lifetime, amazing trip with her friends. Sometimes things are so good, they must be true.

Abundance in your life is as simple as allowing someone to open a door for you. You can practice this anywhere there is a door. A car door, a house door, the door at your local convenience store, at an office building, restaurant – there are so many options available.

- When approaching a door, observe the people near the door. Is there anyone else approaching the door from the inside or the outside?

- Walk your normal pace, or slightly slower. Allow the flow of energy to embrace you and the people around you.

- In your mind or out loud, ask yourself, "Wouldn't it be nice if one of these helpful people opened the door for me?"

- When someone reaches to open the door, look at the person, smile, and say, "Thank you." That is where the energy exchange begins. Their gift to you is opening the door. You complete this part of the energy exchange with your gratitude.

- Feel the gratitude in your heart. You are thanking the person and affirming to the Universe that you are ready to receive.

- Placing your hand on your heart will magnify the feeling.

- As you walk through the open door, imagine you have just walked through a blessing of light and gratitude.

- Thanking the Universe for this helpful person anchors into your body the feeling of gratitude.

- Give thanks for the opportunities that other helpful people will introduce to you.

- Celebrate yourself for welcoming helpful people, better job opportunities, adventures, and loving relationships into your life.

Cynthia Stoneman is a bestselling author, certified mind-body-spirit practitioner, mastery energy healer, oracle and angel card reader, ceremony officiant, and international corporate trainer. Cynthia is blessed with having the words people need to hear, when they need to hear them. She believes that words have power and uses her gift to empower her clients to improve relationships through the power of words.

Her bestselling books include *356 Days of Angel Prayers* and *111 Morning Meditations*.

Cynthia resides in Arizona. Her favorite activities are dancing, going on "Grandmama adventures" with her grandchildren, and road trips with her knight, William.

cynthiastoneman.com

ALL ABOARD! DESTINATION: NEW EARTH

Brandi Strieter

I'd like to invite you on the ride of a lifetime. This journey is unlike anything you've experienced before now. Hold on tight, pack your adventure bags, and welcome to the expansion of the human consciousness.

For over four decades I lived my life through the lens of my ego, only I was completely unaware of its single-sighted perspective. I seemingly fit in the box perfectly, fulfilled my roles and obligations as expected, and found my worthiness in external validation. Can you relate?

I didn't have time to tune into my feelings or emotions, as I was too busy with the never-ending external distractions and competitions for my attention and energy. It was exhausting, I was drained, and eventually my body could no longer keep up.

The only way to describe what happened next is to say that it was the most perfectly orchestrated divine plan meant to move me into a higher vibration. And as we know, before an arrow is propelled forward it must first be pulled back. The same is true for growth and expansion. Breakdown is usually experienced before breakthrough.

When my body manifested disease and I lost all hope of any recovery, I had nowhere left to turn and ultimately faced what I feared the most: myself. No one was coming to save me. I had only myself and it took every single experience that led up to that defining moment for me to go inward. Like the butterfly, I went into a metaphysical cocoon, and there is where I rediscovered my higher self. Soon, however, I was experiencing what felt like an inner tug-of-war between my higher self and my ego, which after so many years of control feared being replaced. It took countless reassurances and a lot of compassion and patience from my higher self before the two could unite and integrate.

Once aligned, the energies intensified and I soon achieved a new level of consciousness. That may sound easy in a story, but I assure you it was anything but. Awakening often comes after what is called The Dark Night of the Soul. As the name suggests, my experience can be described as climbing out of hell or my soul being ripped from my chest. Words simply fall short in describing the anguish and despair I experienced, yet a remarkably and completely unexpected new way of being was also born.

Now, keep in mind that there is no rulebook for when you suddenly hold more light in your body. The higher wisdom, heightened senses, and new gifts may induce the feeling of a mental breakdown, but in reality, it is a quantum leap into a higher level of consciousness. No longer is the world only viewed from a fixed third-dimensional perspective, but now reality can also be experienced through the eyes of unity and compassion. It is in this sacred space that presence, purpose, and unlimited prosperity are achieved.

Stepping into a new way of being (without a guidebook!), I quickly discovered the power of presence. With heightened senses and an increase in overall awareness, I found myself being pulled in a million different directions. The experience reminded me of an antique switchboard. I was learning to plug into many more circuits than were previously available and at times it felt overwhelming.

The journey through the expansion of the human consciousness is becoming the higher self and being connected to Source energy. From an energetic perspective, presence is the door-opener to the magic that awaits. Slowing down, practicing silence, and learning how to become the observer opens up a new timeline of possibilities. Our senses also go on overdrive and a childlike curiosity awakens; life becomes a state of discovery. By grounding, opening the heart center, and connecting with Mother Earth, we are better able to move the high-frequency energies of the expansion through the body so our focus can remain in the present moment, which is where we remember the richness of life. By allowing these moments of experiencing the new and unfamiliar, we expand through love and our life experiences. As one learns to navigate the waves of thoughts and emotions swirling around, while remaining unattached to them yet anchored in the body, a new sense of purpose will begin to take shape

I remember on one of my first desert walks with a higher perspective feeling like I must be hallucinating. Every plant, tree, rock – you name it – was *alive*. Now, of course, to my physical eyes everything appeared familiar, but what I experienced was a higher state of being. I had a remembering of unity, connection, and compassion that was remarkable and I didn't want to go back to my previous frequency. However, Spirit reminded me that I could access this vibration at any time as it was always within me, and all that was needed was for me to be open to and allow Source to flow through me.

I learned that feeling is the first step to healing, and also that the time to release what no longer serves us is now. By shedding any density, more space opens up for the light to enter and as a result, a higher vibration is achieved. This is important because personal vibrations affect the frequency of all of humanity and the entire planet.

What does purpose mean to you? Take a moment now to place your hand on your heart and tune into your divine guidance for the answer. I once thought purpose was my job. Then I thought it was my role, be it as a mother, a wife, an advocate. As you can see, I said "thinking," which indicates my ego was answering the question. With presence and a connection to higher self and source, an expanded view can be accessed. Purpose is not a destination or achievement, rather, purpose is that dream in your heart, that internal knowing that won't go away, and that moment-by-moment experience of living consciously and intentionally.

Personally, I discovered my purpose is to shine a light for others in the darkness, to hold space for healing and to bridge the gap for the awakened. Yes, that description sounds deep, and when I broke it down with Spirit, I was alternatively labeled the "Welcome Committee." I'm still unsure which one I prefer.

As your purpose reveals itself, it's vital to continue to clear and process the shadow aspects of self that are presented. By staying the observer, and not taking things personally, the energy will move through your body with more grace and ease. Know that whatever surfaces, you are supported and guided with love and compassion. It is through this process that awakened beings hold frequency in their bodies for expansion of the human consciousness.

Are you beginning to see the connection between presence and purpose? First, there is awareness, followed by connection and, finally, creation. One comes before the other as they are the building blocks of advanced consciousness. This consciousness houses the energy of prosperity, which is also a frequency that can be tapped into. Think of it like turning a radio dial to a new vibration. However, prosperity cannot be achieved without prosperous thoughts.

As it's been explained, in order to attract said frequency, one must first become that frequency since like attracts similar.

My favorite way to raise my vibration is through gratitude and appreciation. When the energy of appreciation is experienced, it invites in a higher vibration. Moreover, gratitude for anything will help to activate more reasons to feel grateful. A simple daily gratitude practice will assist you with maintaining your vibration and living from a more empowered state. In other words, one will be living a human experience while also simultaneously experiencing life as the higher self. This is the ascension journey in a nutshell.

Everything can appear status quo on the physical plane but energetically the integrated soul is traveling through dimensions and receiving downloads, wisdom, and guidance. There is no match for the frequency of light and love. Manifestation becomes effortless with access to the higher vibrational frequencies and support. No longer are you only creating from the third dimension. With the expansion of the human consciousness, many new tools and shortcuts are available and can be found in the higher dimensions.

A few tips to remember when creating.

- Thoughts to self must mirror what is desired. If your mind is in chaos, so will be your reality; conversely, if your thoughts are in harmony you will receive the similar.

- The law of attraction is real and responds to your vibration, not your intentions. Feeling is the fastest way to bring the experience into reality.

- We create our reality. With awareness comes a conscious choice and then action. One cannot be a victim and victor at the same time.

- Faith is paramount. As the relationship with your higher self deepens, a new confidence is revealed, and any trust is built through consistency and compassion.

- Love is the key and the highest vibration after joy. Open the heart center and invite in abundance for the mind, body, and Spirit.

From one embodied human to another, I honor you for courageously opening yourself up to all that has been reminded of you – everything that is asked of you to grow and expand, the deep dive exploration, the feelings, the frustrations, and the triggers. All of these are what it means to expand the human consciousness. This is the unfolding, shedding, unwinding, and dissecting of you to really understand who you have been and what has been driving your emotions, thoughts, and behaviors, so you can then go inward and keep excavating more.

It's a daily conscious awareness of who you are and why you incarnated on Earth at this time. Remember, you have everything you need inside of you to master your thoughts and step into your highest state of being. Congratulations on your progress, and welcome to the New Earth.

Brandi Strieter M.Ed. has walked an eventful journey through trauma, advocacy, and an eventual chronic disease diagnosis. That journey led her into surrendering … and her ultimate freedom. Brandi has since devoted her life to personal growth and discovered her purpose to shine light for those in the darkness. She now guides those who have awakened to their own light using intuitive guidance, energy and gemstone healing, and the mind, body, Spirit connection, so that she can support those seeking true spiritual alignment. Brandi Strieter is an Ascension Guide, Reiki Master, and Spiritual Teacher. She has mentored under Transformational Thought Leader Sunny Dawn Johnston since 2016 and is proud to be the Community Ambassador in the ELEV8 international membership program. Brandi Strieter resides in Arizona with her family and German Shepherds and enjoys photography, bath meditations, and spending time in nature.

brandistrieter.com

PROSPERITY AS A WAY OF LIFE

Shanda Trofe

I've been a student of Universal Laws for nearly twenty years. I've read countless books, taken multiple courses, and experimented with every manifestation technique possible. At this point in my spiritual voyage, I'd say I live a prosperous life with a thriving business, likeminded clients and colleagues, a loving and supportive husband, and family and friends whom I cherish. Overall, I'd say my life is blessed.

But, it hasn't always been this way. Mine has not been a straight path to the top of the mountain as one might hope when they set out on their journey seeking spiritual enlightenment and a prosperous life. It's been a bittersweet trek with twists and turns, valleys and dips, gains and losses.

When I first learned of the Law of Attraction and discovered the process of manifesting, and realized I create my reality with my thoughts, emotion, vibration and intentions, I was enamored by the instant results I was able to achieve with focused attention. It was as if I'd awakened some innate wisdom I'd always had, just waiting at the brink for me to tap into its power. And oh, how powerful it was!

I remember when I'd first learned the art of visualization and scripting as a means to materialize my desires. I was quickly able to manifest a lump sum of thirty-thousand dollars, which was spent before it could even get comfortable in my bank account, followed quickly by a month when I could barely pay my bills, with even higher gains and devastating losses in the coming years.

How could that be? Looking back, I now know I lacked consistency, held limiting beliefs, and had some deep, inner work to do on my blocks (and deservingness) to abundance. Those are things being a lifetime student of personal development has helped me to overcome... with time.

Ultimately, what I learned through all the inner work and countless hours spent reciting affirmations, visualizing the life of my dreams, and conducting rituals and spells under the moon, is that the simplified path to a prosperous life is not about learning a new technique, trying it until it no longer works, and then moving on to something else. That only breeds internal self-doubt, which lowers vibration and repels abundance.

Living a prosperous life isn't just about the act of manifesting as a morning ritual, or conducting a money spell when we're low on cash. Prosperity is a way of life, and until I started living my life in a way that encompassed positivity, high vibration, and intention, my abundance would come in waves – it, like my actions, lacked consistency.

If I had to take my years of gathered knowledge, training, and experience and simplify it in one chapter of a book (such as this one), this is what I'd share with you: the path to a prosperous life can be achieved by embracing five key components: intention, vibration, belief, release, and consistency.

Intention

The first step to attracting, or tapping into, abundance is getting clear on what you want. It's been said by many gurus, from Tony

Robbins to Michael Beckwith, that "energy flows where intention goes." No matter who originally coined the phrase, there's a reason why so many adopt the adage and live their lives by it. Setting an intention sends your order out into the Universe. There are many techniques to send out that request, and which one you choose is up to you. It could come in the form of a prayer, affirmation, ritual, visualization; it could be as simple as writing your desire on a sticky note or telling it to the moon. It doesn't matter if you're spiritual or religious, if you ask God, the angels, or your preferred deity for assistance. Again, that's your choice. The act of getting clear and stating your intention is what counts – no matter how you go about it – so I always begin there.

Vibration

Like attracts like. Our vibration, emotions, and feelings return to us, like a magnet, that which we are emitting to the Universe. If you want to attract a prosperous life, live as if you're already prosperous. Feel into the energy of prosperity and abundance. And here's a hint: the easiest way is to be grateful for all that you already have, no matter how big or small. Taking time each day to thank God or the Universe, or wherever your faith may lie, for all that you have, and really feel the joy and gratitude in your heart will, in turn, raise your vibration.

While we need to keep our thoughts and emotions as high as possible, that's not always easy to do in life. However, what we can do is any necessary inner work needed to help shift our moods, thoughts, and how we show up in the world. The more we live and act from a place of gratitude, love and joy, the more good will return to us. It's a Universal Law. This is not something you do once, like setting an intention; rather, it's a way you live your daily life.

There are other ways, in addition to gratitude, to lift your vibration. Do something regularly that brings you peace, such as adopt a yoga or meditation practice. Focus on the good in the world instead of the bad, be mindful of what you allow into your energy field by way of the news, social media, and politics. Be mindful of the company you keep and the energy they bring into your space.

It's inevitable that as spiritual beings having a human experience, we are going to find ourselves in a low vibration from time to time. We will experience loss, heartache, and bouts of frustration and anger. We wouldn't be human otherwise. But how we react to events that happen around us is our choice. And by keeping our vibration high, we will, in turn, attracter fewer negative experiences over time.

The goal is to keep yourself in a positive, high vibration the majority of the time, recognize when you need to pivot, and then take action to create change in your environment, mood, and overall emotional state. It's not about becoming perfect, but rather being mindful of your actions and energy.

Belief

One of the main blocks to manifesting abundance and prosperity, at least in my experience, is the deep-rooted belief that it's not going to work, that it's not in the cards for us – in other words, that we don't deserve it. When those limiting beliefs come up, recognize them for what they are: your old stories and blocks to your abundance. Do the necessary work to rewrite those stories and shift your mindset. The best way to do that is to figure out where the belief originated and then decide that it no longer has to be your truth. It was likely learned or ingrained in you at a young age. Once we have the awareness of where our limiting beliefs come from, we can shift them and change the narrative.

Above all, we have to believe that not only can we live a prosperous life, but that it is our birthright, and we deserve it.

Release

There comes a point when we can try too hard, hold too tightly, and that puts a desperate, lack energy out into the Universe that attracts negative experiences back to us. This was the case when my husband and I were trying to purchase our first home. I was self-employed and he was laid off from his job – not exactly a recipe for a smooth mortgage process... or so I convinced myself. We wanted the home so badly that I was growing obsessed with the *how* we were going to make it happen, rather than focusing on the end goal: living our best lives inside our dream home.

To say the homebuying experience was a nightmare is an understatement. While I was able to manifest the down payment and closing costs rather quickly, there were many bumps in the road along the way, right up to the last minute at the closing table. In hindsight, I now realize my constant stress over whether or not we'd get the mortgage was creating one problem and block after another. The Universe was simply responding to my energy and vibration. Had I released the "how" and focused on the end goal instead, it would have likely been a much smoother process.

We must set our intention, keep our vibration high, have belief that we are deserving of it, and release the *how* to the Universe. Always focus on the end goal, for the Universe simply responds to the energy we are emitting.

Consistency

You may think this component contradicts what I just shared about release. And yes, while I believe we must release *how* we are going to acquire all that we desire, that doesn't mean we can lack consistency when it comes to focusing on the outcome we hope to achieve, or being conscious of our words, thoughts, emotions, and actions. It's not up to us to figure out how things are going to happen, but rather, focus on having it as if it is already ours, and living as if it is already here.

Consistency also means doing the work – both the inner work and following the suggestions laid out here – not only as a recipe for manifesting something you are trying to attract, but as a way of life.

To live a prosperous life, we must live every day from a prosperity mindset. It is not so much about learning to *attract* it, but rather to *become* it. We must appreciate all the good around us that is already here for the taking, and do the work each day to keep our vibration high, to shift limiting beliefs, and live in the knowing that not only are we worthy of all we desire, but that it's already ours. When we can do that, we smooth the path to prosperity and make our journey more peaceful, joyful, and blessed.

Transcendent Publishing founder **Shanda Trofe** has been helping writers become bestselling "authorpreneurs" since 2012. Her passion lies in helping her clients turn their message into their life's work by creating viable businesses through authorship. She combines her spiritual training with her writing and publishing experience to guide them and capture their vision, both intuitively and professionally.

Through her various online courses and coaching programs, Shanda specializes in teaching book-writing, self-publishing, and marketing strategies for authors, coaches, healers and entrepreneurs, taking them from idea to publication.

Shanda lives in Florida with her husband and their adored fur babies. You can learn more about her programs and bestselling books at:

shandatrofe.com

THE MAGIC OF AWARENESS

Julie Tufte

One of my earliest memories of "not enough" happened when I was very young. I was with my mom at Dauth's Market, a neighborhood grocer in my small hometown of Paso Robles, California. Mom went to pay for the groceries but came up short on cash. It was after work, she was tired, and needed these few things to feed her family. Being the ever-helpful first-born child that I was, I suggested that she just "pay with a check." She smiled at me – weary, a little embarrassed – and let me know that it didn't work that way. I don't remember what happened after that, I just know that I absorbed that moment directly into my being.

Growing up I never *felt* like we didn't have enough (although looking back I realize Mom must have been a magician). Our house was the one that everyone came to after a game, after a practice, or just to hang out at on the weekends. There was always a meal, a place to stay, a shoulder to cry on, a family if you needed one. Whatever we had, we shared. There wasn't any martyrdom. Giving of our time and, as I now understand, limited monetary resources, was just the way we did things. Lovingly, from the heart, and feeling richer for the experience.

Like most families I knew, we owned a small business in town. However, my stepfather was not a savvy businessman. He was the proverbial big fish in a small town, and in order to remain a big fish he always wanted the bigger house, the newer car, and for sure the next round was on him. Mom's "new" was coming up with new ways to get the bills paid and creatively stretch every dollar. I remember overhearing the "do we pay the employees or pay the bills" arguments. They always left me with a stomachache, unsafe, and confused.

Lurking in the background of our family dynamic was an awareness that money is a struggle. There was never enough. Money was something to outwit because you couldn't count on it. To make ends meet you'd need to work a second job, buy things on layaway, and offer practical gifts for birthdays and holidays. We never talked about it out loud. I never "felt" poor, yet I never "felt" rich, wealthy, or abundant in a monetary sense either. Somehow I always had what I needed and the extras found a way to me as well. I participated in band, student government, vaulting, and cheerleading. We traveled to tournaments and events, hosted holiday dinners and celebrations. And we never turned anyone away.

My household wasn't a particularly religious one. I went to church with my family up until high school. I then opted out, becoming disillusioned by the disconnect between the words and actions of the congregants and the scripture they espoused. The rest of my family continued, but we weren't a pray-before-meals kind of family. For me, I could see the beauty and the blessings co-created with a Higher Source. It was the connection to the everyday miracles that made my heart sing. So the opening of our doors and sharing with our friends wasn't because of some dictate from God or adherence to a strict religious tenet. I believe it was from a deeply-rooted belief that all would be well.

This meant that I grew up in a state of (perceived) financial lack while also knowing, down to my core, that I was prosperous.

In 2009 I was looking to learn something new. I wanted to help people, but didn't know how. I wanted to pick up some skills but was not sure exactly what that meant. This led me to enroll in SWIHA's Mind Body Wellness Practitioner program. There I learned that I had been "life coaching" since I was eight years old. I suddenly had words to explain all the things that I didn't even know had an explanation! The word for feeling all the feels is "empathy," the word for simply knowing things is "claircognizance," and the list goes on. Stumbling into this community gave me a new lease on life and a purposeful direction. Discovering a soul family/ tribe enriched my life in ways that I didn't know was possible.

When my oldest son, Evan, was four years old, he insisted that he wanted to live in the snow. (This was interesting because, in this lifetime, he hadn't yet been to the snow.) After living in Arizona for sixteen years I too was ready to live in a cooler climate and for the next two years I worked hard to find a job that would take us to one. We were so tired of living in the heat, staying cooped up and "refrigerated" half of the year, surrounded by block walls, concrete, and asphalt. This mermaid was ready to move somewhere with grass, trees, and a lot of water. I was combing job sites, filling out applications, interviewing, flying out for site visits, the whole nine-yards. The challenge was that either the job was great but in a place that I didn't resonate with, or the location was amazing but no one followed through on the final hire paperwork. I absolutely believed that I had to get a job secured before we could move anywhere! I mean, that's what a responsible woman with two kids would do…right?

Our desire to move came to a tipping point in 2020, when Phoenix had the hottest summer on record. Evan was attending second grade on a computer in my bedroom and I was busy trying to keep four-year-old Eli out of the way and occupied – all in a seven-hundred-twenty-five-square-foot apartment! That's when the three of us sat down and had several family meetings. It was important to me that we all had a "say" in our future. We talked through what was and wasn't working in our current situation. We explored how we dreamt of spending our time. We imagined how we wanted to feel in our home, community, and surroundings. Our answers pointed us to a small town in the Upper Peninsula of Michigan, a place I had only seen pictures of. There was just something about the trees, the light, and the promise of four (!) seasons that we couldn't resist. Plus, Lake Superior was exactly the body of water I needed. I could hear her calling me.

I did a LOT of praying and meditating. For the first time in decades I remembered my dreams. The trees were asking me what kind of music I was bringing to them. I stood in snowy meadows and could HEAR the snow!! Frozen 2 played on repeat as I couldn't relate to anything more at the time! As all of these experiences revealed themselves, I became very aware that This. Was. Happening.

How were we going to move two thousand miles away... to a place we'd never even been before...only knowing a few people from internet groups... and NO JOB!? Despite these very real concerns, however, my faith was telling me that this move was exactly perfect for us. Instead of letting the monetary aspect determine our path as I had in the past, I was going to follow my knowingness. I did not check one single ad. I did not attend one interview. I decided to go into business with a woman who already lived there. That was risky, sure, but it felt better than any other options. We were just going to show up to our dream. If I looked at it from the outside, I know it sounded insane.

I don't know how to explain the crazy, rollercoaster months that followed, except to say that they were magic. I rose above the financial fears that were programmed into my very existence. I challenged myself to rise above the duality of material lack and soulful abundance. I wrapped myself up in the knowledge that prosperity was already mine. I leaned into the support of my ancestors and Co-Creator, and I knew that we were going where we were meant to be. By following our hearts, imaginations, faith in the Universe and one another, we were headed into our next adventure.

I won't pretend that everyone understood or supported our plan, or that I didn't have a few meltdowns along the way. When you step out into your dreams, it triggers a lot of people. It gives them a chance to look at their own fears, regrets, and programming. Often people project their issues onto you. Of course that gave me the incredible opportunity to dig deep and see what was mine and what wasn't. It gave me time to heal wounds and recognize those that still needed work. Memories from my own childhood were brought front and center.

The most important part of this whole process was including my boys. Together we examined our priorities. We worked through what was required to make the necessary changes to step into alignment with them. I was keenly aware that this was a once-in-a-lifetime opportunity to walk the talk like never before. THIS was living in prosperity!!

I've come to understand that prosperity is the *magic of awareness*. An awareness that you live amongst good and wondrous things. When you surround yourself with – and strive to become – grace, beauty, love, and compassion, you transcend the traditional idea that prosperity has anything to do with the state of your finances. When you are able to pinpoint the things that you are grateful FOR and appreciative OF, you know the true ingredients of your prosperity. It only gets better from there, because then you can start working with the magical energy of prosperity to achieve your hopes and dreams.

Julie Tufte is a Mind-Body Wellness Practitioner, Therapeutic Bodyworker and Intuitive Wellness Coach. She combines her training as a Clinically Certified Hypnotherapist, life coach, reflexologist, and toe reader with her intuitive abilities and love for all things chakra-related. Her passion is to help people connect the dots between their emotional and physical bodies, and is called to empower those around her to find their personal truth and healing.

Out of all the titles Julie has earned, "Mom" is the one she treasures most. She is a solo parent to Evan and Eli (and cats Hamper and Pico). Raising her boys to embrace their gifts is an honor and a privilege. Originally from the Central Coast of California, Julie spent almost twenty years in Arizona before the family moved to the UP of Michigan. There they enjoy a most prosperous life, reveling in the magic of Lake Superior, surrounding nature, and fantastic community.

POWER OF THE MIND
Amie Wade

I would like to write this chapter with the excitement of telling you that I'm a multimillionaire and have all the answers, tips, and tricks on how to become one yourself. I would love to tell you that I'm financially secure and debt-free and that I've traveled the world and had adventurous experiences. Well, I can't tell you that I've done all of this… yet… however, it has occurred in my imagination.

Everything that has been created began with a thought, an idea. This must mean that for something to come to fruition I first have to see it in my mind. Absolutely! But this is only a piece of the process.

Most of my life I've lived with the mindset that I was unlovable and not good enough. The experiences that contributed to this way of thinking were abandonment, abuse, and molestation, which all led me to contemplate suicide. These painful experiences stacked on top of one another, created an emotional heaviness and I just wanted to end it all. I didn't want to continue living if all I was meant to do was to feel these heavy emotions and then take my last breath at whatever age that may be. Why would anyone want to live life that way?

I am an observant person. I developed this skill in my childhood – be seen and not heard. And it wasn't safe to use my voice in a way of speaking up for myself – especially if it meant expressing what I didn't like. Feeling safe was a concern. After being molested at age fourteen, a lot of anger set in, and the self-defeating thoughts got louder. In my teens and twenties, I noticed how many people, especially the adults, did not express much joy. Many people harbored sadness, grief, and anger. It was a time when "keeping up with the Joneses" was a thing, with people trying to outdo their neighbors, friends, or family members with material objects, no matter how much debt they incurred. And even though they had all the stuff, their happiness level was still very low.

Money didn't grow on trees for my family, and you had to work hard to get it. I also learned that even if I got all the money I wanted, I wouldn't be happy, because money doesn't buy happiness. That said, I would need money to pay for all my necessities (shelter, food, clothing, utilities, etc.) and for any extracurricular activities (travel, eating out, going to the movies, getting my hair done). It seemed people either had money but no time to enjoy it, or all the time in the world and no money.

What is it about this paper that I put so much value on? There's so much attention that I give to money but don't give to myself. At some point I had determined that my value was based on what other people thought of me and I have lived in accordance to that. If I pleased and affirmed **them** and **they** were happy, then I felt accepted and loved and that was very valuable to me. I had the belief that love was something that came from other people. It was evident that my biological father didn't love me since he left before I was born. My two abusive stepfathers didn't love me, or did they? Was the abuse their expression of love?

Love comes in many forms. A mother loves her child "unconditionally," as long as they put their clothes in the hamper, get good grades, and give no back-talk. The intimate relationship that fills the void in the heart with the love that wasn't received in childhood, only to be diminished from disappointment when they don't meet your expectations any longer. The love of the new car that has been worked so hard for, until it breaks down or has a flat tire and the whole day is ruined. Love is a tricky thing when it is expected to come from a source outside of yourself.

Then there's the deciding factor of worth. Am I worthy of receiving an abundant amount of love and prosperity? I believed that I wasn't. I did some bad things and made some bad choices, and that made me believe I was a bad person. This programming was instilled in my mind in childhood. Just for incarnating, I wasn't worthy. For not getting it "right" as a child, and then being yelled at, affirmed that I wasn't worthy. If I'm not worthy as a child, then I won't be worthy as an adult! Life was stacked against me. So why the hell am I here on this planet? I wasn't a fan of "life."

I observed people around me. I heard their painful stories and felt their anger. And even though the situation had occurred many years prior, they chose to hang onto it. Is that what we are supposed to do – store all this pain inside our minds and bodies forever? Yes, if you want to and no if you don't want to – it's a choice.

Imagine if you will that you want to go up in a hot air balloon. You want to rise above the trees to see the incredible view. The ropes tethered to the basket must be released and the balloon must be filled with hot air to help it rise up. If the basket is tethered it will only rise a short distance above the ground. Now, think about wanting to be successful and prosperous. Think about the stories of the past and all the heavy emotions that come with them. Think about all the limiting beliefs, the unhealthy habits, and patterns that you have. Each one represents a rope that is attached to you, keeping you from rising to the person you want to be and receive that which you desire. One by one, you must release that which binds you in the way that you have been to become the person you want to be.

A mindset shift is required.

If you have the belief that you must work hard to get what you want, then most likely you will continue to work hard all your life, get what you want, be too exhausted to enjoy the fruits of your labor, and continue to work hard toward the next best thing. Each time sparks a glimmer of happiness, but does not sustain it because, again, you're expecting something external to fill a void that resides within you. If worthiness is an issue, it doesn't matter how many material objects you get, how many loving and healthy relationships you have, or how much excess money is in the bank, you will find a way to sabotage yourself and maintain the limitations on how much goodness you allow yourself to have.

You are worthy just because you exist.

Being prosperous is a sign of well-being; well-being is being of good health; good health is an indicator of how you think. Your thoughts are followed by emotions; emotions effect the physical body. Negative thinking activates stress hormones and inflammatory agents. Stress is the number one cause of most dis-eases. Positive thoughts spark good feeling emotions and stimulates the body to produce natural healing chemicals. Thoughts, words, and emotions are all energy, and you get to choose which type of energy you want to feed within yourself.

God created all that is good. And here you are!

If you're reading this book in the hopes of getting the secrets to having prosperity, let me share with you that the solution lies **within you**. What do you need to do? Get out of your own way! Turn your attention inward and connect with the true essence of all that you are. You came from an infinite source, where there is no lack of anything and an abundance of everything. This abundance could ignite love and joy, or you could attract an abundance of something that leads to anger, sadness and hopelessness.

You get what you focus on.

You came from a Source of love, which means you are already love and loved. Life experiences have created distance between you and your spirit – they have dimmed your light – and it's up to you to fill in the gap. To love yourself. Listen, it's no one's job to love you; it's no one's job to make you happy. This is your responsibility. It's your choice. Maybe you need to have permission to be happy, to feel worthy of prosperity, to feel loved. Actually, **you need to give yourself permission** to receive all the goodness that you deserve. All I and anyone else can do is to encourage you.

You need to hold the vision and stay focused on that which you **want** to bring into your life. Here's some guidelines of how to do it:

- Clarity and focus. Be clear about what you want and focus on it as if it's already happened. You have the money; the bank account balances are consistently increasing; you're driving the new car; you're enjoying your dream house; you have the business or job that fulfills you. Use your fun and playful imagination.

- Feel it now! As you are using your creative imagination, experience in your body the emotions and physical sensation that you'll have when you do have the manifestation. If you want to have a beach vacation, then in your mind see yourself on the beach, feel the breeze and the warmth of the sun on your skin; hear the birds and waves; feel the relaxation, peace, and calmness; the smile on your face. You may feel a sense of relief and security because there's an overflowing amount of money in the bank account to pay for the vacation. And maybe there's joy as your intimate partner sits on the beach with you.

- Momentum. Look at pictures of the beach, decide where you want to go, and investigate travel arrangements. Create some momentum in the direction of having the beach vacation. When you are visualizing what you want, you are sending that information to the Universe. It's a co-creation, teamwork.

- Allow and receive. When your manifestation comes to fruition there are two words that you need to be very good at saying – and they are, "Thank you!" Practice this now! Say thank you when someone buys you lunch or coffee; when receiving a gift or compliment; when receiving a hug; or any kind gesture toward you – all of it! For a while, practice nothing more than saying "Thank You!" with a smile on your face.

- Enjoy your manifestation!

The mind is a powerful tool that needs to be intentionally utilized.

Prosperity is everywhere, waiting for you to embrace it. It's up to you to release the past that you've been grasping and be open to receive the most amazing gifts intended for you. **You deserve it!**

Amie Wade is a Certified Life Coach; Certified Mindy, Body, Spirit Practitioner; Reiki Master/Teacher; Certified Angel Card Reader; and certified 200-hour yoga teacher.

Her childhood stories of abandonment, abuse, and molestation were contributing factors of feeling hopelessness and having suicidal thoughts almost daily. As an adult, she used alcohol to cope with her unhealthy emotions and as a way to be able to relax and have fun. With the information she gained from taking the certification courses and listening to a multitude of spiritual teachers and influencers, she learned to change her perspective about her life experiences and released her alcohol addiction.

While working full-time in the corporate world, Amie dabbled in coaching for fifteen years with her Reiki clients and the classes/workshops that she facilitated. She decided that her desire and mission is to help guide women on their healing journey so they can be resilient in living a spiritually empowered life with a deep sense of self-love and, therefore, established her business as Amie Wade – Emotional Resiliency Coach, LLC.

amiewade.com

LOVE CREATES PROSPERITY
Jennifer Wheeler

"Jennifer, when you love, you love with all that you are," my mentor in college told me on a call one day. When he said it, I felt like someone finally understood me, even if only for a brief moment in time.

To me, prosperity is about the people I have manifested to help me create the life I want to live. They weren't always people I realized I needed. Sometimes what I learned was so subtle it took me years before I recognized the lessons. Sometimes the people didn't behave in the manner I wanted them to, and sometimes it took me years to create the relationships I desired. No matter what the case, each one is valuable to me.

My parents had a very volatile and angry relationship, which left me making promises to myself at a young age that I would never marry anyone I didn't love with all my heart, and that my children would never feel like I did. It wasn't always an easy road, and I may not have always made the best decisions. In my relationships I never felt I could really trust anyone with my heart. I never really felt loved, and I never loved anyone, not the way my heart wanted to. I was afraid to be alone so I always stayed too long and felt like I was settling. My inner desire to be with my soulmate won out over every mistake I made. I now know I needed these lessons so I could learn how to be the person my soulmate needed me to be.

I learned about being a good woman, wife, and mother from my stepmother. She took the time to talk to me about love. She told me how grateful she was when she met my dad, that he was her best friend and they truly loved each other. More than that, she showed me by the way she lived her life how to love someone. I could see it in all of the little loving things they did for each other. Her actions showed me how important it was to let other people know you love them. Life is precious, so you should always say I love you because there may not be another chance. Though as a hurt child I couldn't always see it, I am, and always will be, grateful to her for teaching me what love is – and for showing me how much she loved me.

My mother taught me the importance of being your own person and that love is all that matters; she believed in a higher power and helped me define my own beliefs. The way my mother viewed things resonated with my soul. She taught me how to visualize, create, and manifest. Mom helped me learn how to love myself and, most importantly, to be alone with me; she showed me that I was worthy of love. Yet I was always searching for my true love, but forgetting to start with myself.

My mother was a free spirit, she was as intuitive as she was rebellious and strong-willed (I come by it honestly!). Her long, flowing red hair was a symbol of her individuality and strength. My mother dared to be different and she didn't let society dictate how she lived and loved; she didn't care what anyone thought of her. The world my mom lived in was filled with enchantment, imagination, just the magic of life. She allowed space for the mystical, the fantasy, but, most importantly, the sacred. I loved that about her. It was the way she viewed the world, and how she lived in this world that made her so magical to me. I was lucky enough that she taught me her magic.

I would often ask her if she thought I would ever find my soulmate. Her answer would always be the same: "Honey, it will be when you least expect it." I would laugh and say there will never be a time when I don't expect it. Mom told me to write to my soulmate. She journaled every day and was always encouraging me to do so too. I never thought of myself as a writer but I liked her idea, and over the course of a few years I would write to the love of my life. My letters would discuss what I was doing with my time and how I wished he was there with me. I saved those letters and eventually presented them to him on our first anniversary.

I spent countless hours creating and visualizing scenarios in which we would meet, and I also created a general description of him. I created scenarios of how our life would be and things we would do and the things we would have in common. Every night before I fell asleep I would imagine a meeting and sometimes it would be a story that would run for days at a time. I would continue it every time I had free brain time, whenever I could let my mind wander.

Filled with hope and the promise of happiness for the future, I was inspired to become a flight attendant. My mom and I had a regular back-and-forth that went something like this. Mom: "Why don't you date a pilot?" Me: "No, Mom, pilots can't be trusted. They all cheat." Mom, laughing: "They don't *all* cheat." I would insist that they do, and she would let it go. My mother was a beautiful soul, and when she died of cancer in May 2005, she left me with a wealth of beautiful memories, including those conversations. I miss her every day and am so grateful that we were able to spend this time together.

Two weeks after she passed, I met Ted – a serendipitous encounter over a box of Krispy Kreme doughnuts. It was my first work trip since Mom's death, it was his last trip for this airline, and we had a long layover in Calgary. I thought it was hilarious that an airbus pilot had a sticker that read, "If it ain't Boeing I ain't going," and said so. That was it. We instantly felt comfortable talking with each other.

We spent the day hanging out with another flight attendant in Banff, who wasted no time in telling me how she had noticed the chemistry between us. Every free moment on the flight to Phoenix we were in the back galley, with the other flight attendant going on about how Ted really liked me, and me replying that I didn't date pilots, she was very interested in us getting together. It was like she was channeling my mom! Ted called me that night and we set up our first real date. That was seventeen years ago, and I have talked to him every day since.

On our first date we sat and talked for hours; I didn't mean to, but I spent almost the whole time talking about my mom. Ted sat there and listened, happy to let me talk about her. This was just his way.

I felt seen and heard with him, and there was a calmness and a gentleness about him that I instinctively trusted. Trust wasn't a feeling I knew very well but it was safe, peaceful, and right where I needed to be. It was the feeling I had been searching for my whole life and that feeling has never gone away. Our wedding day and the birth of our daughter are my favorite memories. Ted is my very best friend, my lover, the place where I still feel safe; he is just as I imagined, only even better. I knew he was out there somewhere, from the time I was little, and I knew it was what I wanted most out of this life.

I know without a doubt that my mother was wherever she is, stirring up her magic to help us get together. And she was right: he came when I least expected it but when I needed him most.

One of my favorite memories of our daughter Maggie began years before we even tried to conceive. Ted and I were standing in front of the departure screen at Phoenix Sky Harbor Airport, choosing a city to go to on an impromptu trip. We settled on Albuquerque, hopped on the flight, rented a car, and spent the day driving and exploring. It was wonderful. During our travels, the song "My Magdalena" came on. I was flabbergasted. Magdalena was the road I had lived on when I met Ted, the first house that had felt like home to me in a very long time. It was also the place where my mom had stayed when she was sick and held some of my last memories of her. The name Magdalena reminds me of Mary Magdalene, and my mother's name was Mary, so it was a way of honoring my mother. Also, as a kid I was convinced my parents named me after Jennifer Lane – the road we lived on – and Ted and I both liked the idea of naming our daughter the same way.

Choosing a name turned out to be far easier than getting pregnant; we ended up trying for over a year. I used much of the same process to manifest Magdalena as I did Ted. I dreamed daily of what a wonderful and loving child she would be. I imagined how she would be outgoing and friendly and everyone would adore her. I imagined her having beautiful blue eyes like her daddy. I went to sleep with visions of this child running through my dreams. I imagined the type of relationship I would have with her and how smart she would be. Instead of writing letters to her, I created a vision board where her father and I each wrote a little note asking her to come join our family. I put it in our bedroom where we could look at it every day, and when she was born she was everything I had imagined and more, just like her father had been. I eventually had that vision board framed and hung it in her room.

My stepmom taught me what it meant to love others and my mom taught me how to love myself. My daughter and my husband taught me that I really am magical and can create the life I desire and to always follow my dreams. They are my prosperity.

Once upon a decade ago, a girl met the love of her life through the most divine circumstances. As a believer in all things magical, she and the fam followed the fairies to the land of yellow warmth, basking in the Arizona sun. Always up for a new adventure, she loves to travel with her family and she finds much joy in exploring new places with the two people she loves the most.

Jennifer Wheeler loves combining creativity and her intuitive gifts to help others. She allows her imagination the freedom to create from the heart. She is passionate about allowing children to nurture their gifts, imagination and, most importantly, the belief that anything is possible.

A BARN, A TREE, AND ME
Bobbi Williams

"Though I cannot flee

From the world of corruption,

I can prepare tea

With water from a mountain stream

And put my heart to rest." –Ueda Akinara

I took a deep breath, stepped back from the buzz words I knew, and even taught about Prosperity. Energetically, "Possibility" felt truer than "Prosperity." "Appreciation" felt truer than "Abundance." Simple shifts to bring me current.

The Secret taught me and countless others about the Law of Attraction, Prosperity, and Abundance; however, today's world is vastly different from the one we inhabited in 2006 when the movie was released. We are now being called upon to up our game. Suddenly denial, spiritual bypassing, and magical thinking were weeds in my soul's garden. It was time to dig out what was not aligning with the constant benevolent power of support I felt in my life.

I chose to review my life, to see what gifts, good and bad, have been given to me to put me on the spiritual path that has brought me so much meaning and goodness. I want to live in this world of change at the spoke of the wheel, regardless of what spins around me.

A teacher of mine once said, "Reset your life, clean out your home, discover evidence of who you were as a child." For me, that was as simple as remembering a sunlit barn and a tree.

As a child, I lived in two worlds. Most of the year our Chicago home was a Greystone owned by my grandparents. My parents were divorced, and my mother, my sister and I lived with them so they could help with childcare. It was my grandmother's lavish bridge club parties for her friends, referred to as "The Girls," that introduced me to an upbeat opulent vibration. Candies and Cashews were in bowls. Drinks, peach cobbler, ham, macaroni and cheese, vegetable trays. In addition, The Girls, though elderly, would arrive with dishes of food, laughing and hugging. They proceeded to chat away, their words punctuated with more laughter as they played cards long past my bedtime.

My grandmother appreciated fine clothes and professional friends. She was a self-made woman, and the first in our family to own real estate. She had also had her share of challenges; for example, her first husband, who she had married at just fifteen, was an undertaker – and abusive. Grandaddy, her second husband, was a kind gentle man, a widower. He came from a prominent family in Maryland.

Gram did her best to make sure we had opportunities she did not have growing up, including sending us to a private Episcopalian grammar school. This was the world she created for us.

Our other world was the countryside. Every summer until I was seven, my grandparents would take us to a home built in Laytonsville, Maryland by my grandfather's great-grandfather. It was here that Mother Nature held me close to her, to safely explore and play. It was as if She was whispering comforting ways to see the world.

I discovered that the sunlit barn was a sanctuary full of creative possibilities. I did not stop at creating mud concoctions, but also found delight in presenting a Daddy Long Legs spider to my sister, who evened the score by telling me ghost stories at night.

I would return daily to the sunlit barn. Long shadows of late summer, sunlight flickering through slats landing on my shoulders. I did not realize that I was absorbing knowledge of how beautiful this world is.

It was, I believe, the genesis of my spiritual journey.

My mother married my stepfather, Jimmy, when I was seven. Jimmy was very wise and had a huge heart. He was an intellectual with rural honesty – I would say a country gentleman. He was perfectly at home relaxing in his overalls, unique in an urban setting. He also enjoyed hunting and country music. He was the best father I could have imagined.

Jimmy was the perfect addition to explore the two worlds I grew up in. He took us boating, and brought our first dog home – a German Shorthaired Pointer we named Fritz. Jimmy had a country road in his heart and a dog by his side. He brought love of the land into our city home.

Both of my parents appreciated the magic of the soul's journey. My mother was an artist who painted mostly landscapes and portraits. She went through a spiritual art phase and produced a series of happy pastel amorphous people. One painting predicted my husband coming into my life; she painted a likeness of him standing next to me, twenty years before we met!

Jimmy had books about Edgar Cayce, psychic discoveries behind the Iron Curtain, and psycho-cybernetics, all of which helped create an opening for me to appreciate that which could not be seen with physical eyes. After many years, medical school, then business school, and the bumps of life lessons, I became a spiritual counselor, a return to exploring the unseen – something that felt like home.

> "Walk to the sun
> and the shadows
> will fall behind you."
>
> –Maori Proverb

I reflect now on how Jimmy once mentioned the sunlight flickering through the leaves of a tree. I was astonished, as I'd seen that very image in a vivid dream earlier that day. Jimmy and I had a soul connection.

The tree became my symbol of prosperity. The further along I went on the spiritual path, the more I reached to Nature. I transitioned from Reiki to Shamanism, the upper realms to Mother Earth.

The tree is firmly rooted. Grounded. Its leaves reach the Heavens and receive the Light from the Sun. Its leaves dance with the Wind. When I want to be reminded of Abundance, I look at the leaves. You cannot count them, but each leaf represents possibility. The tree is timeless and wise from history, all it has seen and endured. And yet it thrives, year after year. All of our human struggles come and go. Our joys and triumphs, come and go. The tree remains silent and strong, connecting Heaven and Earth.

As a girl, I also knew the walks with my sister down the country roads held the magic of trees. I was in awe of honeysuckles (she taught me to suck them), homemade blackberry wine my grandfather let me sip, and the chickens and cows. The trees stood by, watching me grow up. Now I am humbled by their powerful spiritual presence.

Unity Church is where I adopted metaphysical Christianity. It embraced many paths to God, all religions. It also impressed upon me the unity of all things, the interconnectedness of all energy. It connected spirituality with nature, a foundation for my eventual shamanic work.

The words Prosperity, Abundance, Spirit, are just our attempts at defining an energy that has always been and will always be. It is a benevolent energy that responds when we open to it. It has a double reach. When we reach for it, it reaches back two-fold. We are the only beings that have been given the gift of creating our worlds. We co-create with Spirit. When we can do so without attachment to the outcome, we surrender to "this or something better."

At Unity Church, I learned a Prayer of Abundance that powerfully opens a portal to receive. Abundance is right in front of you always.

> "I dwell in the midst of Infinite Abundance.
> The Abundance of God is my Infinite Source.
> The River of Life never stops flowing and it
> flows through me with lavish expression.
> Good comes to me through unexpected avenues
> and God works in a myriad of ways to bless me.
> I now open my mind to receive my good.
> Nothing is too good to be true.
> Nothing is too wonderful to have happen.
> With God as my Source nothing amazes me.
> I give freely and fearlessly into Life.
> And Life gives back to me with fabulous increase.
> I Am indeed grateful. And so it is."
> –Author Unknown

Saying this prayer brings me tremendous serenity.

A Prosperity teacher, Edweine Gaines, once said the Prosperous Power of the Universe is like electricity. It is always present, you just need to plug into the outlet. Also, like electricity, it has existed throughout time, we just needed to evolve to discover it!

Of the many classes I taught at Unity Church, one of my favorites was "Live the Life you Love" based on the Law of Attraction. The Law of Attraction had often been minimalized by focusing on material wealth, but its power is much greater and more fulfilling than this. In my spiritual counselor certification training, I learned the future is an illusion. It is here, right now, in our choices.

So where does serendipity fall into this? It is a bonus. Once we choose, "this or something better" shows up. Prosperity, in all its forms, was a state of being in awe of what is possible to create.

Here is an example: I practiced real estate part-time. I also created a home-staging business. One day, I affirmed three times out loud "Opportunities are coming to me Now," each time followed by a clap. Within a half hour I received a call I almost did not answer because I did not recognize the number. It was Realtor Magazine asking me to be part of an article featuring three realtors demonstrating and competing with their staging abilities – an incredible opportunity. Our staged home office won and we were featured on the July 2006 cover! From that, Crain's Chicago Business called for an interview!

Recently, I was hospitalized for three days for a severe intestinal inflammation and found myself thoroughly enjoying my stay. I discovered a TV channel of sunrises from all over the world. I relaxed watching a Costa Rican jungle, Stone Henge, and other habitats' birds and animals awaken to the rising sun. I felt the constant strength of stones, the movement of life. Long after our daily noise is done, the Earth will go on. I recognized a spiritual gift:

Nature making me whole, healing. The nursing staff commented on how they loved visiting my room. Abundance is right in front of me.

The real essence of prosperity is the knowing that God, the Universe, Spirit – whatever name you give it – has your back. It is the support and magic of the unseen. It is the force that brings serendipity and grace while you create your life. It says, "You pick, walk down that road. There are unexpected treasures here." There is healing. Most of all, there is a love of life created from the knowledge that all is well, all will heal. Steadfast, just like the tree. There is a Divine Goodness that, even in our darkest times, lights a way. It is the brightest vibration of Love.

1 Corinthians 13:12 says:

> Now we see but a poor reflection as in a mirror; then we shall see face to face. Now I know in part; then I shall know fully, even as I am fully known. And now these three remain: faith, hope, and love. But the greatest of these is love.

I was in high school when I posted this bible verse on my mirror. I still see my journey in these words today.

Bobbi Williams is a Certified Spiritual Counselor from the American Institute of Healthcare Professionals, a Reiki Master Teacher, a Certified Psychic/Medium Investigator, and a Registered Neurodiagnostic Technologist. She founded "Home for the Soul" based on architect Anthony Lawlor's book and tagline "From the moment we are born, we seek to find Home." Bobbi, who holds an MBA from the University of Chicago concentrating in Behavioral Science, previously worked as a hospital administrator. She also has taught many classes at Unity Church and created workshops on many spiritual topics.

Bobbi has co-authored chapters in *Navigating the Pandemic: Stories of Hope and Resilience,* and in the Amazon bestseller *Wild Woman's Book of Shadows* under the pen name as Esme Chamane, meaning "Beloved Shaman."

She lives with her husband and two dogs in Chicago.

For further contact information and bookings go to:

home4thesoul.com.

INNER PEACE IS CURRENCY

Alesha Anne Wilson

"If it costs you your peace, it's too expensive."
~ Paulo Coelho

Every day, I take risks that increase the possibility of my loved ones saying they've finally had enough (of my boundaries and my seeming inflexibility) and decide to revoke my open invitations to gatherings. Though these risks are completely self-serving, most of the time I experience discomfort. What in the blazes could be worth the risk of not belonging and voluntary uneasiness?

The answer is both simple and complicated: inner peace.

My first experience of inner peace occurred when I was five years old. Standing at the bottom of the steps leading up to a three-story building, I had an uncontrollable urge to cry and beg my mother to take me to a different school. I couldn't explain it, I just knew it felt unsettling and that I didn't belong there. Since that was over forty-three years ago, I'll most likely never know what that three-story building had in store for me, but I can tell you I was at peace with where I ended up.

Several years later, after a relatively successful freshman high school year, I asked my parents to transfer me to another school even though it meant I wouldn't be a cheerleader and I would be leaving behind the closest friends I'd had to date. Though the feeling didn't bring me to tears, the nudge to move was strong, and luckily my parents agreed without a fight. At the time, I wasn't aware that the Universe was supporting me, but I knew from experience that expressing my intuitions eventually led to feelings of calmness, confidence, and love. During that sophomore year, I was to meet my husband.

I can't say whether I knew that baseball player was going to be my husband, but I know his certainty of our relationship scared me; plus, the long-distance area code almost doomed it from the start. My inner peace was in need of attention once more and, as I mentioned earlier, does not come without risks. When I ended up transferring back for the second semester and leaving him without saying goodbye, I knew I could be risking losing an important part of my future. I also thought that at fifteen years old I needed experiences that a steady boyfriend would get in the way of.

Somewhere along my travels, I picked up the notion that things were not supposed to come easily. I never believed that hard work alone was going to help me achieve goals, yet I ended up on the bandwagon, starting to ignore my intuition because it seemed too easy. Plus, it was hard to ignore the struggles of those around me. I felt like a total oddball with my rose-colored glasses. If you cannot relate to the phrase, "The struggle is real" you probably know what I'm talking about. Eventually, I decided to give misery some company and allowed the doubts and fears of my surroundings to slowly deplete my currency. Deplete my inner peace.

After my risky sophomore farewell, I embarked on adventures that left my intuition sitting on the bench a majority of the time. It happened so frequently that it took a car accident at the end of my junior year to bring me back to awareness. After spending the summer recovering from a broken jaw, hip, and femur, that ball-player called unexpectedly to share his own derailed path that led back to me.

I realize that I have navigated most of my life with a hybrid version of inner peace. For years, I asked the Universe to help me be the person I needed to be for myself, my family, and others – and for the most part I have felt prosperous as a daughter, sister, wife, mother, teacher, counselor, business-owner, et cetera; however, I still longed for the authentic, magical inner peace I felt as a child. I missed the freedom and ease that seemed to be a part of the process. The frustrations I felt when I ignored even the smallest of internal nudges and pulls felt real, but unnecessary. They felt unnecessary given my choice to ignore my intuition.

Transforming my spirituality, reading self-help books, and journaling have been a part of my daily routine for over twenty years. I still carry with me the saints and guardians from my Catholic upbringing, the tolerance of attending friends' churches that didn't align with my beliefs, and the magic that is found in admitting I only know a fraction of what is out there.

About five years ago, I came across one of Maya Angelou's quotes, "You are only free when you realize you belong no place – you belong every place – no place at all. The price is high. The reward is great." I immediately felt a strong connection with those words. It felt like my soul was making an agreement without my conscious consent. I already had experience making high-stakes decisions such as letting go of adult friendships that drained my inner peace, telling my husband that our future looked bleak given our physical trajectories, and declining events and situations that didn't feel right even though I was expected to attend. Yet, Maya's words seemed to ask for more. To me, this meant learning to pay even more attention to my power of intuition. But first I needed to learn how to appreciate myself and my potential on a deeper level.

The suggestions I offer do not necessarily come with much risk, but they may lead to truths that are risky to share with others who do not have the same belief as you. For example, my use of oracle card readings, human design, chakra meditations, and crystals, isn't something that everyone will agree with, but they are tools I use to help me become aware of my expansive intuition.

Here are some of the rituals, practices, and routines I've utilized on my continued journey towards inner peace:

- Expressions of Gratitude. I started a daily practice of writing three to five things I am thankful for. This practice developed into writing up to twenty things a day, writing a "one hundred things I love about my husband" book, and starting to verbalize my gratitude to others throughout the day. Eventually, my self-talk transformed into the language of love and light that seems to fill my cup full with inner peace. I've had a little help these past four years, since medical marijuana became legal in Oklahoma, with having the ability to slow down and smell the roses. Cannabis helps me experience pain relief, which is optimal for relaxing and recharging. It also shows me what it feels like to have a quiet mind and the ability to witness the world with wonder and authenticity.

- Trust that you know. Trust that you know the best foods for your body, the best way to exercise, the best place of employment, relationships, et cetera — regardless of what others say. For years I tried to seek outside myself for the best diet/workout routine but my energy drained just thinking about them. Eventually I gave into the constant nudge that told me that my morning coffee was restricting weight loss. Then I went back to the basics of my gymnastics training and added floor toning exercises (because they helped me get a kick-ass, strong body back then). This process would not be possible without heavy doses of gratitude and grace.

- Avoid falling into the trap of praise by others. Learn to trust the validation of following your own path. If you feel drawn to give in because of the possibility someone will say "You're the best," just know it will get easier the more you practice saying, "I love opportunities to help out, but this time it doesn't work for me." I used to think all I needed was praise from others, but when I became aware of the negative dialogue within, I realized that mindset was depleting.

- Transform your responses. For so many years, I thought it was my obligation to ease any tension with an apology. But the more I replaced "I'm sorry" with "Pardon me," I noticed a transformation of my mindset. I no longer felt it was my duty to apologize for being anywhere. I belong every place. Pay attention to any phrases you say that start an internal negative dialogue. This is a sign that you are not responding in your highest good. The more I practice, the easier it is to speak up before the dialogue begins.

- Meditate. There are so many ways to meditate, but I was guided toward resources on mindfulness meditations which gave me the confidence to keep trying. I encourage checking out the recent documentaries on the subject to see if it sparks anything – but pay attention to signs and synchronicities that lead to what works for you. It took me a good three months before I felt comfortable recommending meditations. I don't like to recommend anything to others unless I've experienced the benefits myself.

- Own your desires. My desires have transformed as I have seen the possibilities of what my truth reveals. I expected to lose weight because of my desire to live a long and vibrant life, but I never imagined my truth to reveal a toned body, short shorts, and cowboy boots this close to fifty. As you share your desires with others, you will encounter many who will not understand your decisions. They will share their doubts, fears, and judgments – you don't need to add your own. Developing a practice of grace is necessary during those times. As long as I am in the pursuit of inner peace, I have made an agreement with myself to have grace. So, when I fall behind on exercise, I give myself permission to ignore any negative internal dialogue because it serves no purpose other than creating a game inside my head.

- Continue your pursuit to see love and light when so many in the world will not or cannot see it yet. Very similar to my gratitude practice, my commitment to seeking the positive started out small and has incrementally grown into something I recognized as a child – the wonder of things.

I used to think that inner peace required me to transform my ideas and wishes into something that worked for the greater good of others. Now, I realize that honoring my intuition, my truth, is for the greater good because my intuition leads me to the powerful love and light of authenticity that the world needs more than ever. Even though my focus is not on others, it feels good knowing that when I have an abundance of inner peace, my loved ones and all those I encounter will benefit from my prosperity.

My earliest memories are filled with happiness. I believe that is because my parents and sister didn't force me to live outside of my design. Since a very young age, my family allowed me to have a voice which later developed into a sense of strength and leadership.

As I entered school, I joined gymnastics, cheerleading, singing, and leadership groups like FBLA. With curiosity for a better self, I found my sense of direction and through it all – wife, mother, teacher, parent educator, counselor, broker, cannabis therapy consultant, free-lance writer – I've tried to use my voice to educate and inspire. Ultimately, my desire for love and light has led me to where I am.

Today, you see me in a given point in time. Tomorrow, I'll be different. The voice to my best self is always with me.

–Alesha Anne Wilson

urbanhippiealchemist.com

PRACTICAL PROSPERITY
Becky Woods

There is so much information about manifesting and prosperity it can leave many overwhelmed and wondering where to start. Allow me to assist you. I will share thought-provoking details that will get your wheels turning followed by practical steps to build a strong manifesting foundation for prosperity. It is never too late to start co-creating your dream life. The Universe doesn't have timelines and limits. What you think should take years to accomplish, the Universe can do in a moment.

The first steps to manifesting your dream reality are to "define and align." Let's start by defining a few of the words I will be using throughout this chapter. First, feel free to replace the word Universe with God, Source, Higher Self, or whatever is your belief of a higher knowing power. Next, let's look at the word prosperity. Prosperity is defined as the condition of being successful or thriving, flourishing, and enjoying vigorous growth. In the bible it is not spoken of as merely the accumulation of wealth, but rather an ongoing state of success that touches every area of life.

A few words that stand out to me in these definitions are *state* and *condition*. A state is defined as a particular condition someone, or something is in at a *specific* time. Condition is defined as: 1.) The state of something, regarding appearance, quality, or working order;

and 2.) The circumstances affecting the way in which people live or work.

The first thing I would like you to ponder is how these definitions are open to everyone's unique interpretation. This means everyone is *allowed* their own definition of prosperity. The next thought I'd like to introduce to you is that prosperity is a *state* that can change anytime, as often as you wish. I encourage you to *expect* and *allow* your ideal prosperity to be fluid and malleable. After all, what is important to us today can be trivial tomorrow.

When we embrace the individualities of prosperity, we can release comparison. When we release comparison, we also release judgment. We afford others the *respect* of *not assuming* we know better than they do, what's in their best interests. This allows us to live a life free of others' judgment and of judging others. Living life free of comparison and judgment is a major game-changer.

I hope you can see how limitless creating your ideal reality and prosperity is. I find it helpful to brainstorm about it in a journal using questions as prompts, for example: Where are you living in this ideal reality? Why did you choose this place? What do you do there? Are there other people there? What kind of feelings does this place invoke within you? Remember, this can change anytime, so have fun and daydream a little.

Once you have started defining your prosperity it's time to talk about alignment. Alignment is energetically lining up with your desires. This encompasses your thoughts, words, beliefs, actions, and habits. I need to take a minute here to talk about conditioning.

Conditioning is the process of training a person or animal to behave in a certain way or to accept certain circumstances. Many studies have reported that ages zero to eight are our formative years because they set the basis for our overall success in life. We learn more quickly than at any other time, and experience rapid intellectual, social, physical, and emotional development. On a collective level, the formative years are considered very important as they present the best chance to mold children and influence future prosperity, inclusiveness, and social stability.

If you are a parent like me, you are probably saying, "OH Shit!" Fear not – we do the best we can with the tools we have at the time, and so did our parents and ancestors. So please hear me when I say conditioning is not a blame game. It is simply a means for us to heal and understand ourselves better. Knowledge is power.

We can trace many of our beliefs, habits, thoughts, emotions, actions, and words back to this formative time. We obviously didn't know we were literally imprinting a permanent recording of what went on around us onto our nervous system. How many times have you repeated phrases that your grandparents used? I'm willing to bet you don't even know what they all mean. One of my grandmother's sayings was "Merciful Minerva!" I just researched that a couple years ago which means that for forty-some years I said it without any idea where it came from or what it conveyed.

Understanding our conditioning is a key to unlocking our potential and allows us to transform it into limitless probabilities. It allows us to ask questions, i.e, *Where did this belief come from? Do I really believe this to be true?* If not, you can change it, and this starts to reprogram your nervous system. *Why do I get stressed out about this?* You might find it's because you witnessed others being stressed about it. *Do I want to continue to respond to it this way?* If not, you can make another choice! It's that simple and that profound.

To achieve and maintain alignment you need to pay attention to your feelings and thoughts. Automatic thoughts, words, emotions, and actions are often a product of our conditioning. Question these. First, gut feelings are often the product of our inner self. When our habits, words, thoughts, or actions don't line up with our inner self, there is discord. This often feels uncomfortable in some way. Think of a time when you witnessed something that you knew was wrong and you were uncomfortable. Most likely it was because you wanted to do or say something. This was your body telling you that what you were seeing was not in alignment with your inner beliefs. If you are having a tough time discerning what is in alignment and what isn't I have a process for you to try. Close your eyes and put your hand on your heart. Take a few deep breaths. Now ask yourself if this is in alignment. You will most times hear a yes or no instantly in your mind or you will feel a warm fuzzy or uncomfortable feeling in your body. Trust this.

It's also imperative that you evaluate your habits. This is a big one. They can point out areas of disbelief or self-sabotage. Let's say your goal is to become debt-free, so you start a savings account. You are faithfully putting money in your savings account each month. Likewise, you are adding more debt to your credit card. These habits are not in alignment with each other and therefore are not in alignment with your desire. This can play out in any area of your life. Adjust your habits to be in alignment with your goals. Most often you know what needs adjusting because you will feel uncomfortable. Whenever you feel uncomfortable or "off," stop and tune into your body. Ask yourself a couple simple questions. Why am I feeling this? Where could I possibly be out of alignment with a belief or goal? Being present, in tune with your body or self-aware is a practice that will change the way you navigate life.

The next steps to manifesting your prosperous reality are to have faith and anticipate. In order to manifest something, you must believe and have faith that you can and will receive it. This is one of the reasons we need to be flexible with our desires. Many times, we desire things and deep down don't believe we can ever have it. This means your desire is out of alignment with your beliefs. No worries, we just adjust a little bit. Let's take a few steps back until we find a desire we believe is achievable. Start there. Once that desire is achieved, move on to the next step. Let's say you desire a brand-new sports car. Your current reality is that you live paycheck to paycheck with an economy car that is paid off. There is always that free raffle you may win and, trust me, it can happen. For many of us, this is too far-fetched for us to believe possible. So, take a few steps back. Choose to manifest the down payment. Choose to manifest a higher-paying job. Choose to manifest a classic sports car that costs less. Get creative. Remember, this is fluid, and you will be re-evaluating and adjusting as you go. If you can believe it is possible, it is a good place to start.

The last piece to prosperity is anticipation. Anticipation is the sitting in excitement and expectation of something happening. Can you feel the difference between anticipation and waiting? There is a high vibe energy to anticipation. You know it is coming! You just don't know when or how. You are excited to see how it all unfolds. I have seen some amazing things along my manifesting journey. The Universe can make things appear out of thin air. It feels quite magical and surreal.

When you first start manifesting, one of the hardest things to learn is to let go of the when and how. That requires faith and trust. It requires you letting go of your ego. Believing that the Universe knows the best way and best time for everything. The easiest way to learn to trust the Universe is to practice. The more things you manifest, the easier it will become. To practice, start manifesting little things that aren't that important to you. Before you leave the house, ask the Universe to grant you front-row parking. Be confident that you will find an awesome parking spot. Pretty soon, you will have front-row parking everywhere you go!

The Universe doesn't differentiate little things from big things. Only we do that. For the Universe to grant you a parking spot is the same as granting you a sports car. That's why the work is ours to define, align, have faith, and anticipate. I hope you found this information inspiring and helpful, and that you use it to go forward and co-create your amazing prosperous life with intention.

I wish you happiness, health, safety, and love all the days of your life. I wish you ease and grace in all you do. I wish you more prosperity than you can carry so that you can share it with others. Remember, as Aristotle said, "Knowing yourself is the beginning of all wisdom."

Amen, Aho, and So It Is!

Becky Woods is a bestselling author, intuitive coach, and Reiki Master. She is also trained in multiple modalities, has an Associate of Applied Science degree, and has been a medical laboratory technician for almost twenty years. One of Becky's specialties is balancing, aligning, and cleansing energies. She does this by intuitively tuning in to energies and then using a combination of her scientific knowledge, medical knowledge, and energy modalities to alchemize dis-ease into ease. Becky is passionate about teaching and empowering her clients to maintain a state of energy ease in all areas of their lives. She feels a special calling to work with children, teens, parents, and veterans and is an advocate for mental health and overall wellness. Her other passion is teaching people how to manifest their ideal prosperous reality. She has been a master of manifesting since she was a small child. See how well you are aligned with your prosperity by taking the free quiz on her website:

energeezinc.com

Thank you for reading our stories, hearing our words, and embracing our rituals. Thank you for awakening the wild woman and fueling her passion and desire to express, create, and live a mystical life rich with community and sisterhood. Together we rise and celebrate each woman – WE ALL GET TO WIN. If you wish to continue the journey, we would be honored to have you join our sacred online space:

bit.ly/WWProsperityBook

CPSIA information can be obtained
at www.ICGtesting.com
Printed in the USA
BVHW032043101022
649105BV00005B/14